Girls' Identities and Experiences of Oppression in Schools

This book uses an intersectional approach to explore the ways in which girls and adults in school systems hold multiple realities, negotiate tensions, cultivate hope and resilience, resist oppression, and envision transformation.

Rooted in the voices and lived experiences of girls and educators, Brinkman, Brinkman and Hamilton document girl-led activism within and outside schools, and explore how adults working with girls can contribute toward their thriving. Girls' narratives are considered through an intersectionality framework, in which gender identity, race, ethnicity, social class, sexual orientation, and other aspects of social identity intersect to inform girls' lived experiences. Exploring data and interviews collected over a 15-year period, the authors set out a three-part structure to outline how girls engage in strategies to enact resilience, resistance, and transformation. Part one reconceptualizes traditional definitions of resilience and documents girls' experiences of oppression within schools, identifying common stereotypes about girls and examining the complexity of girls' "choices" within systems that they do not feel they can change. Part two highlights girls' active resistance to stereotypes, pressures to conform, and interpersonal and systemic discrimination, from entitlement of their boy peers to experiences of sexualization in school. Part three illuminates pathways for educational transformation, creating new possibilities for educational practices.

Offering a range of pedagogies, policies, and practices educators can adopt to engage in systemic change, this is fascinating reading for professionals such as educators, counsellors, social workers, and policy makers, as well as academics and students in social, developmental, and educational psychology.

Britney G. Brinkman, PhD, is an interdisciplinary researcher, educator, licensed Psychologist, and an associate professor of psychology. She works extensively with schools and community organizations to promote justice for girls. She is the recipient of a Citizen Psychologist Presidential Citation from the American Psychological Association and is the author of *Detection and Prevention of Identity-Based Bullying: Social Justice Perspectives*.

Kandie Brinkman, PhD, is an independent researcher and educator at various local universities and high schools, teaching social change along with forming multiple community-based projects and committees. She is the recipient of the University of Utah's Martin Luther King Award, as well as multiple citations for her work in social justice. Her passion is to empower girls and women.

Deanna Hamilton, PhD, is an associate professor in the graduate psychology programs at Chatham University, Pennsylvania, US, where she teaches courses in lifespan development, psychopathology and resilience, and positive psychology. She integrates positive psychology research and interventions in her courses. Her published papers explore strengths, well-being, and self-efficacy across a variety of domains.

Girls' Identities and Experiences of Oppression in Schools

Resilience, Resistance, and Transformation

Britney G. Brinkman, Kandie Brinkman
and Deanna Hamilton

Routledge
Taylor & Francis Group
LONDON AND NEW YORK

Cover image: Getty

First published 2022
by Routledge
4 Park Square, Milton Park, Abingdon, Oxon OX14 4RN

and by Routledge
605 Third Avenue, New York, NY 10158

Routledge is an imprint of the Taylor & Francis Group, an informa business

British Library Cataloguing-in-Publication Data
A catalogue record for this book is available from the British Library

Library of Congress Cataloging-in-Publication Data
A catalog record has been requested for this book

ISBN: 978-0-367-62946-5 (hbk)
ISBN: 978-0-367-62944-1 (pbk)
ISBN: 978-1-003-11153-5 (ebk)

DOI: 10.4324/9781003111535

Typeset in Sabon
by Taylor & Francis Books

Dedicated to all girls who dare to dream.

To my family, friends, students, and colleagues – your thoughtfulness and our discussions helped shape many of the ideas in this book. And, to Mike, for all the love and support. I am the luckiest.

For my granddaughters, Emmeline and Thessaly, as they grow into strong young women.

Contents

Acknowledgments

This book would not have been possible without the assistance and support of many wonderful people. First, we express our deepest gratitude to the girls and educators who shared their stories with us. Without their bravery and willingness to reflect on their experiences in schools, this book would not exist.

We want to thank the school administrators, principals, and teachers who supported this project and allowed us entrance into their schools and classrooms.

We are grateful to the editors and staff at Routledge Press for making this book come to fruition. We appreciate the generosity of the Society for the Psychological Study for Social Issues, whose funding supported the research in the second phase of our project.

So many people assisted with the research and development of this book. Thank you to all members of the Psychology of Gender Research Team at Chatham University, and the Social Justice Psychology Research Team at Point Park University. Countless graduate and undergraduate research students allowed this work to flourish through implementing workshops and collecting and analyzing data. We are especially thankful to the research assistants who helped with this project including: Allison Jedinak, Keely Hirsch, Aliya Khan, Kate Mead, Meredith Deal, and Isabella Yobbagy. We are grateful to Edward Dinnen, Sean McGreevey, and Elizabeth Bennett for meticulously reading chapters of the book and providing us with excellent feedback. A special thank you to Miles Dinnen for editing. Thank you all for braving even the very rough drafts.

This project is the culmination of 15 years of work dedicated to understanding girls' experiences within schools and striving to create environments in which they can thrive. It was built with courage, love, and perseverance. We are so grateful to all of our friends and family members who encouraged us as we worked on this project and who support us in all the work we do to improve the lives of young people.

Introduction

Can you think about a time you were treated differently because you were a girl?

The school sits back from the street, almost hidden away. You might have a hard time finding the entrance if you did not know it was there. As with many Catholic K-8 schools, St. Bernadette Catholic School[1] is attached to a church building. The school is small, with one class per grade, but like most elementary and middle schools, the building is full of life. Next door sits Christ the King Catholic High School. The school was established in 1921, but the main school building is older and once was the site of a hospital. In the mornings and afternoons, the entire block is teeming with activity as students file in and out of both schools. These two schools became the site of our longitudinal research study exploring girls' experiences of sexism in school. We later returned to the high school, along with other schools in the same Catholic School system to conduct a follow-up study to understand how girls' experiences of sexism and other forms of oppression in schools evolved over time.

This book examines how girls and adults in school systems hold multiple realities, negotiate tensions, cultivate hope and resilience, resist oppression, and envision transformation. We investigate this by exploring data collected about girls' experiences of oppression in school spanning more than a decade. We describe how three processes—resilience, resistance, and transformation—are intertwined and inform each other. Resilience in the face of oppressive systems is essential for girls' survival. However, we assert that educators and professionals working with girls should invest in creating environments that promote thriving for girls, not merely survival. Girls engage in active resistance to others' definitions of them, pressures to conform, and interpersonal and systemic discrimination. Girls also strive for transformation of unjust systems for themselves and others. We explore how adults working with girls make sense of and can contribute to girls' efforts toward thriving.

We situate our explorations of girls' experiences of oppression in schools with the foundational understanding that educational systems—particularly

DOI: 10.4324/9781003111535-1

within the United States—are designed to reinforce existing systems of inequality. Most current educational systems dehumanize both marginalized and privileged youth—forcing all children into environments that create limitations on what is allowed and what is valued (Ayers, 2016). Our work is embedded in critiques of the white, patriarchal, capitalistic models of education rampant throughout the US and globally, offered by scholars like Paulo Friere (1970), bell hooks (1994), Monique Morris (2019), Venus Evans-Winters (2005), Bettina Love (2019), and others. These systems are microcosms of society—they were designed to uphold and reinforce the inequalities that exist within society. Thus, exploring girls' experiences in schools can illuminate how girls experience society, how they make sense of their identities, and how they navigate oppression.

We view girls as complex, agentic individuals, navigating complicated educational, social, and cultural dynamics. We are particularly interested in understanding girls' experiences of oppression related to gender; however, it is essential to scrutinize oppression from an intersectional lens. Intersectionality theory provides a framework for understanding how social identities interact, inform the construction of each other, and are experienced by individuals and communities (Collins, 2015; Collins and Bilge, 2016; Crenshaw, 1991). This theory can be utilized as an analytical tool for exploring differences within social groups and commonalities across groups. We view girls through an intersectionality framework, in which gender identity, race/ ethnicity, social class, sexual orientation, and other aspects of social identity intersect to inform girls' lived experiences. Intersectionality can also challenge structural inequities and reductionist approaches to social identity (Cole, 2008). We employ intersectionality as a practice for engaging with the complexities of social identities and locations within structures of power, privilege, and oppression (Brinkman and Donohoe, 2020; Cole, 2017). Throughout the book, we seek to nuance our conversations about girls' experiences through the lens of intersectionality and the recognition that there are commonalities and differences in individual girls' lived experiences related to their other social identities. Further, we conceptualize girls as active agents in their identity development processes. Girls do not unilaterally respond to experiences of oppression, nor are they "blank slates" who internalize oppression. Girls engage in dynamic negotiations of external pressures to conform to stereotypical expectations about their identities with their preferences and perceptions of self, all within interpersonal, social, and political contexts (Brinkman et al., 2014).

The book is rooted in the voices and lived experiences of girls and adults in schools as told to us through in-depth interviews. Our intent is not to offer one narrative about "girls' experiences" or easy solutions to address oppression in schools. We sought to listen deeply to our participants, to recognize their experiences as fluid and complex, and to amplify their inner voices amidst the noise and chaos that often surrounded them. We worked to resist our own desires to simplify any one individual or narrative. Rather, we strived to hold tensions as they arose in our data—to allow conflicting and contradictory narratives to emerge, to hold multiple realities, perspectives, and methods for meaning-making. We agree with Gonick et al. (2009) who argue for "complex theorizations of gendered agency and resistance that illuminate what is enabling and constraining and how femininities are contingent and ambiguous" (p. 6). We designed the research studies described in this book to create space to hear what we didn't know; to challenge our preconceptions; and to allow for confusion, frustrations, contradictions, as well as joys, surprises, and hope. We recognize as Ahmed (2017) states, "There is no guarantee that in struggling for justice we ourselves will be just. We have to hesitate, to temper the strength of our tendencies with doubts" (p. 7). Our own experiences of conducting the research and writing this book mirror the complexities expressed by our participants—throughout this process, we have felt curiosity, helplessness, despair, inspiration, anger, pride, and hope.

We invite you as readers to explore the complexities of girls' lived experiences. We encourage you to look for and engage with the nuances, complexities, and contradictions that arise as girls and educators describe their experiences in schools. We situate the experiences of our participants within existing literature about girls' school lives and also recognize that our book cannot be (nor is it intended to be) a comprehensive account. Our intention is for this work to be a catalyst for conversation—we hope you leave the book with more questions and curiosity, an openness to deeper understanding of girls' experiences of oppression in schools, and motivation to create expansive possibilities for educational spaces.

The Schools

We conducted our research studies[2] within a Catholic School system in the Western United States, where one author (Kandie Brinkman) has worked as an educator for 25 years. We also draw upon research across many different types of schools and apply our findings broadly. We recognize that some of the dynamics we encountered are particular to Catholic schools and recognize that girls' experiences in other school systems have similarities and differences.

What is the difference between a Catholic school, a private school, and a public school? Often stated as the "Catholic School Difference," Catholic Schools offer a Christ-Centered education that infuses faith and values-based learning environments with a sense of belonging and a commitment to justice. According to the United States Conference of Catholic Bishops, parochial schools in America are a historical consequence of racism and alienation of the 19th century. Irish Catholic immigrants who were taunted and harmed by the Know-Nothing Party—later known as the KKK—were the earliest enrolled into Catholic Schools due to alienation from local public schools. In the late 19th and early 20th centuries, schools widened their mission to embrace disenfranchised Native American and African American children in urban areas. During the early founding of Catholic education, the schools were staffed by women and men who belonged to religious orders, and this continued up to the mid-twentieth century (United States Conference of Catholic Bishops). Today, Catholic Schools are under the direction of either a parish or the local bishop. In 2022 Catholic schools are mostly if not entirely staffed by laity (non-ordained individuals). Catholic schools are private, religious-based educational institutions with a core mission and value system. Schools often cite that Christian values and academic excellence go hand-in-hand. The overall mission is to serve God by providing a challenging academic education rooted in Catholic values and morals in developing the whole person.

We gathered data from girls and educators from four different Catholic Schools over more than a decade of time collected in two phases. The first phase was a six-year longitudinal intervention and research study exploring girls' experiences of sexism conducted at two schools, St. Bernadette Catholic School and Christ the King Catholic High School. Both schools in Phase 1 were located in an urban area with a majority White (73%) population. Latinx individuals are 13% of the population, Asian individuals are 13%, and Black or African American individuals make up only 2%. The mean income for men is $41,247 and women earn a mean income of $32,406.

Our first school was St. Bernadette's, a small inner city parish K-8 grade school with only one classroom for each grade. During the time of our study, the parish priest and all teaching staff were White, and most teachers were female, with one male teacher, and the principal was a lay White woman. The second school, Christ the King, is an inner city Catholic High School (grades 9–12) with an average of 850 students and 35 faculty and staff members. Approximately 60–70% of the student population identified as Catholic. The school population is the second most diverse in the state, including Latinx students and African immigrant students. LGBTQ and non-binary students were present in the student population, although there was no public record of demographic information regarding gender identity and sexual orientation of the student body. At the time of our study, both male and female administrators, including vice principals and deans, made up the administrative staff. Two different White men served as principals during the time we conducted our longitudinal research study.

The second phase of our project included interviews with girls and educators. We collected data from students and educators at one new research site—Our Lady of Guadalupe—and from educators at Christ the King and St. Martin de Porres. Our Lady of Guadalupe Catholic High School is a suburban school, connected to a K-8 Catholic school. The school is located in a region that is predominantly White (90%), with Latinx families representing 7%, Asian families representing 4%, and

Black or African American families are only 0.75% of the population. Men make an average of $73,694 while women earn an average of $41,191. The school sits on a large complex established in 1999. The majority of students identified as White, upper middle class with about 60% self-identified as Catholic. About 5% of the student body identified as students of color, most identified as Latinx. LGBTQ and non-binary students were present in the student population, although there was not a public record of demographic information regarding gender identity and sexual orientation of the student body. At the time of data collection, there was an all-White and all-male administration at this research site, including the principal and vice principal, the development director, campus life director, activities director, and dean of students. There were no women in the administration team. There were 50 faculty and staff members at Our Lady of Guadalupe, and all but two identified as White. Among the teaching staff, the male-to-female ratio was close to 50/50.

St. Martin de Porres is a parish school located in a less-affluent area of a major city in the western United States. The racial makeup of the county is 60% White, 32% Latinx, 2% Asian, 2% Pacific Islander, 0.89% Black, 0.79% Native American and 2% from two or more races. Founded in the early 1960s, the school didn't become K-8 until 1993. At the time of our study, the majority of students were low income with both state and diocesan financial aid.

Our Research Studies

The initial longitudinal study conducted at St. Bernadette's began with an invitation. Would we be willing to create an intervention to support the girls in the 6th grade? The school principal was concerned about how the boys were treating the girls and wanted to offer the girls programming to support them. At that time (2004), there was a growing dialogue within the United States (and internationally) about empowering girls and young women. Programs such as Girl Power (a national public health effort sponsored by the U.S. Department of Health and Human Services) and Girls' Incorporated offered community-based programs designed to empower young women with resiliency skills in the areas of education, life choices, and health.

The dominant narratives of "girl empowerment" programs at the time fell short for us. They consisted too much of the premise that adults (usually women) would teach girls that sexism exists, that they should resist it, and that their lives would then magically be transformed. We were concerned that this approach over-simplified girls' experiences. Some of these programs emphasized girls' "voices," but most focused on how girls lose their voices or ways they are victimized. The "at-risk" framework can present girls as helpless objects of their own stories (Harris, 2004). While we wanted to support girls' empowerment, we also wanted to contribute to scholarship examining girls' roles in their own empowerment and self-understanding (Kearney, 2009).

We developed a program that would teach girls about sexism and offer them tools to be resilient while also developing a research project that allowed us to learn from the girls about how they were already coping, surviving, and thriving. Our intervention was a gender-transformative program—these programs teach people to think critically about, and work on, challenging gender inequalities (Barker et al., 2007; Brush and Miller, 2019). Gender-transformative programs have been found to improve men's and women's health and are highly promising as a type of public health strategy (Barker et al. 2007; Miller, 2018). This programming approach emphasizes teaching critical thinking skills to support youth in recognizing the detrimental impacts of rigid gender roles. Gender-transformative interventions for children can be effective at decreasing girls' adherence to rigid gender norms (Brinkman et al., 2010). We worked with the same group of girls from 6th through 11th grade. During their 6th-, 7th-, and 8th-grade years the girls participated in four workshops per year on topics including gender prejudice and sexism, relational aggression, and body image. In high school, additional workshops were offered on cyberbullying, healthy relationships, and media literacy.

During the intervention, we conducted a longitudinal exploratory study examining girls' experiences of sexism and their development of resilience and resistance to structural inequalities. The girls participated in interviews at the end of each school year in which they talked about their experiences of gender prejudice and how they responded, their attitudes and beliefs about gender roles, experiences of sexism within the classroom, how gender dynamics influenced their relationships with family and friends, romantic relationships, career goals, and their beliefs about themselves. The number of participants fluctuated yearly. The largest number of participants in a given year was 11 girls (6th grade). Thirteen girls participated during their middle school years. Four girls participated in middle school and high school. A total of 36 interviews were collected over the six-year period.

In 2017 we conducted the second phase of the project and included students and educators from the same school district in the western United States where the longitudinal data was collected. We interviewed 19 adolescents (11th and 12th graders) and ten educators from the various schools. The names of all of the participants and schools in both studies have been changed to pseudonyms to protect their identities. (See Appendices A and B for detailed information about the participants.)

About The Authors

We enter this work as three women informed by our own lived experiences as girls, by our work with girls (as teachers, therapists, and researchers), and our own experiences of oppression within the same systems we seek to understand and transform. Phase 1 was designed and implemented by Dr. Kandie

Brinkman and Dr. Britney Brinkman. In 2016 Dr. Deanna Hamilton joined our research project, and together, the three of us designed Phase 2. Undergraduate and graduate research assistants worked on our team throughout both studies, assisting with implementing workshops, collecting data, analyzing data, and coding qualitative data.

Britney G. Brinkman, PhD

I am an associate professor of psychology and a licensed psychologist. I have worked extensively with girls in schools, in community organizations, and through clinical practice. My research agenda has focused on understanding how children, adolescents, and young adults construct, making meaning of, and navigate their intersecting social identities. I also examine factors influencing adolescents' and young adults' involvement in activism, advocacy, and social change work. I prefer to conduct research from a community-based, participatory-action framework in which I work collaboratively with community members to develop a project that will address questions or problems that they care about. I agree with Fassinger and Morrow (2013) who argue that "research can be used to either perpetuate or disrupt the social status quo, to oppress or empower marginalized groups, to provide an experience that blames people for their victimization or seeks to liberate them and transform their lives" (p. 70). It is my intention with this project—as with all of my research—to use the tools of the research process to support the liberation and transformation of girls' lives.

I come to this book with my own former experiences as a girl who attended Catholic schools and who was known for engaging in resistance when I felt that something happening in school was unjust. There were many points along this journey where I could resonate with the experiences girls shared with us. I often found myself surprised and disappointed by the elements of oppression in school that had not changed since I was a child—the pressures to be smart but not outshine boys, the expectations to be "good," the rampant sexual violence, the limited room for transformative work. My goal throughout this project was to listen deeply to girls about their lives in school—to stay open to hearing their struggles and accomplishments, to allowing space for nuance and unanswered questions within their narratives.

Kandie Brinkman, PhD

Over the many years of my professional career I taught in a Women's Studies Program at a local university, teaching social change and forming multiple community-based projects and committees. Concurrently, I taught theology in two different Catholic high schools. Pulling together my academic orientation with my Catholic faith, I outlined this project as part of my hope to discover the strength of both Catholic education and its positive impact on, and outcome for, girls. As a veteran educator teaching social justice, leading diversity clubs, and always interacting with young women, I wondered if there was a better tool kit for these girls. Out of this desire and curiosity, this project was born, and I became this project's community partner. I wondered if Catholic education allowed faculty to develop a more justice-oriented curriculum, as well as a school inclusive—and better yet, nurturing—of students "growing up girl."

Deanna Hamilton, PhD

I am an associate professor of psychology trained in clinical and developmental psychology. I have taught developmental psychology to graduate level counseling students for over 15 years, and I have taught and done research in the area of positive psychology throughout my career. I come to this book having been, largely, ignorant and unaware of resistance and advocacy as a girl and adolescent. School served as my source of solace and place for achievement, and I was exceptionally committed to being a "people pleaser." Hearing the stories of our participants made me (as a woman firmly in middle age) feel both hopeful for continued advancement in how we think about and support empowered, healthy development in girls and sad and frustrated about a lack of progress (and in some cases, worsening conditions) in the decades since I was a girl.

My intentions going into the research and the writing of the book were at least three-fold (some were certainly better than others): 1) to return to working with and hearing girls' stories. My academic career has involved working with college students (primarily graduate students), and I was craving hearing about girls' experiences in their voices; 2) although I did not have many preconceived hypotheses about what we would hear, I did suspect that it would be more nuanced, sophisticated, and complex than the way that girls and the constructs we explored (resilience, resistance, transformation) are often given credit for or are described; and 3) to learn how to write a book and to add a book to my professional development. I am aware of how lucky and privileged I am to get to do this with such amazing and brilliant women!

Resilience, Resistance, and Transformation

Part 1 of the book is dedicated to resilience—we describe the psychological literature about resilience and ways that educational systems engage with the language of resilience. We examine narratives and expectations regarding three categories of girls: the *Good Girl,* the *Smart Girl,* and the *Super Girl.* These labels are often considered indicators of girls' resilience and evidence that girls are doing well within our educational systems. We argue that pressures to conform to these constructs create and reinforce sexist, classist, racist, and homophobic attitudes and hold girls to unreasonable expectations, often leading to considerable distress and consequences to girls' well-being. We also recognize that girls' resilience is rooted in efforts to survive oppressive systems and cultures. Conforming to others' expectations, to school rules, and to dominant discourses of femininity can be forms of resilience (at least in the short term), helping girls survive in problematic systems. When living in oppressive systems that girls cannot change, it might be most protective of their sense of self and their understanding of their own safety to reframe the situation as less harmful. We offer explorations of alternative models of resilience as it intersects with healing and recovery.

In Part 2 of the book, we turn our focus to resistance. We describe a range of strategies girls use to resist stereotypes about femininity and experiences of sexism, from labeling sexist events to confronting perpetrators of interpersonal sexism. We also situate girls' resistance within the context of their schools and the larger sociopolitical context. The longitudinal nature of our project allowed us a unique opportunity to document how trends in education and the social context regarding masculinity shifted over time and impacted girls' experiences. In the early 2000s when we began our initial study, narratives about a perceived "boys' crisis" in education were common in the United States and globally. These arguments often asserted (despite data to the contrary) that boys were falling behind girls in school and that schools were intentionally designed to hinder boys' development. Over time, we saw how this assertion that boys were being left behind morphed into aggrieved entitlement—a feeling that one's manhood has been threatened and the belief that one is entitled to get it back, even through violent means (Kalish and Kimmel, 2010). We examine how fragile and toxic masculinity impact girls' experiences in school and their resistance to oppression. We describe how schools are built to support and privilege boys, often protecting them from scrutiny and positioning girls as second-class citizens who must simultaneously be more mature than boys but also less visible. We detail how the intersection of White privilege and male privilege created a toxic and unsafe environment for girls and all students of color.

We also scrutinize how girls navigate contradictory expectations regarding sexuality in which girls are sexualized (Renold and Ringrose, 2013) while also being punished for their sexuality (Raby, 2012). We analyze the mechanisms in schools that reinforce the sexualization of girls and promote sexual violence, creating dangerous environments for girls. We assert that dress code policies and enforcement practices simultaneously sexualize girls while also policing their bodies through hyper-surveillance. We document girls' resistance strategies to sexualization and sexual violence within schools.

In the final section of the book, we explore pathways for transformation of educational systems. Mission statements and strategic plans often include promises of envisioning new futures for education but rarely deconstruct existing hierarchies of power. In this book, we dig deeper to examine pathways for meaningful transformation. We elevate ways girls are already engaged in transformative work within schools through their activism. We elucidate the need to offer opportunities for healing for educators and describe a range of pedagogies, policies, and practices offering pathways for transformation. We envision educational systems as having the potential to be places where girls (and all students) can thrive. We seek to generate dialogues that are expansive in understanding girls' experiences—to catalyze conversations that hold complexities, ask questions, and create new possibilities for educational practices.

Note

1 All names of schools and participants have been changed to pseudonyms.
2 The research studies described in this book were approved by Institutional Review Boards at the authors' institutions. Participants completed consent and assent forms agreeing to participate in the study.

References

Ahmed, S. (2016). *Living a feminist life*. Duke University Press.

Ayers, B. (2016). *Demand the impossible!: A radical manifesto*. Haymarket Books.

Barker, G., Ricardo, C., Nascimento, M., and World Health Organization. (2007). *Engaging men and boys in changing gender-based inequity in health: Evidence from programme interventions*.

Brinkman, B.G. and Donohoe, P. (2020). Doing Intersectionality in Social Justice Oriented Clinical Training. In *Training and Education in Professional Psychology*.

Brinkman, B.G., Rabenstein, K., Rosén, L., and Zimmerman, T. (2014) Children's Gender Identity Development: A Dynamic Negotiation between Conformity and Authenticity. *Youth and Society*, 46, 835–852. doi:10.1177/0044118X12455025.

Brinkman, B.G., Jedinak, A., Rosén, L.A., and Zimmerman, T.S. (2010). Teaching children fairness, decreasing gender prejudice amongst 5th graders. *Analyses of Social Issues and Public Policy*, 10, 171–191. doi:10.1111/j.1530-2415.2010.01222.x.

Brush, L.D. and Miller, E. (2019). Trouble in paradigm: "Gender transformative" programming in violence prevention. *Violence Against Women*, 25(14), 1635–1656. doi:10.1177/1077801219872551.

Cole, E.R. (2009). Intersectionality and research in psychology. *American Psychologist*, 64, 170–180. doi:10.1037/a0014564.

Collins, P.H. (2000). *Black feminist thought: Knowledge, consciousness, and the politics of empowerment* (2nd ed.). Routledge. doi:10.4324/9780203900055.

Collins, P.H. and Bilge, S. (2016). *Intersectionality*. Polity Press.

Crenshaw, K. (1991). Mapping the Margins: Intersectionality, identity politics, and violence against women of color. *Stanford Law Review*, 43, 1241–1299.

Evans-Winters, V.E. (2005). *Teaching black girls: Resiliency in urban classrooms* (Vol. 279). Peter Lang.

Fassinger, R. and Morrow, S.L. (2013). Toward best practices in quantitative, qualitative, and mixed-method research: A social justice perspective. *Journal for Social Action in Counseling & Psychology*, 5(2), 69–83.

Freire, P. (1970). *Pedagogy of the oppressed.* Continuum.

Gonick, M., Renold, E., Ringrose, J., and Weems, L. (2009). Rethinking agency and resistance: What comes after girl power? *Girlhood Studies*, 2(2), 1–9. doi:10.3167/ghs.2009.020202.

Harris, A. (2004). *Future Girl: Young Women in the Twenty-First Century.* Routledge.

hooks, b. (1994). *Teaching to transgress: Education as the practice of freedom.*

Kalish, R. and Kimmel, M. (2010). Suicide by mass murder: Masculinity, aggrieved entitlement, and rampage school shootings. *Health Sociology Review*, 19(4), 451–464. doi:10.5172/hesr.2010.19.4.451.

Kearney, M.C. (2009). Coalescing: The development of girls' studies. *NWSA Journal*, 1–28.

Love, B.L. (2019). We want to do more than survive: Abolitionist teaching and the pursuit of educational freedom. Beacon Press.

Miller, E. (2018). Reclaiming gender and power in sexual violence prevention in adolescence. *Violence Against Women*, 24(15), 1785–1793.

Morris, M. (2016). *Pushout: The criminalization of Black girls in schools.* The New Press.

Raby, R. (2012). *School rules: Obedience, discipline, and elusive democracy.* University of Toronto Press.

Renold, E. and Ringrose, J. (2013). Feminisms re-figuring 'sexualisation', sexuality and 'the girl'. *Feminist Theory*, 14(3), 247–254.

Chapter 1

What Is Resilience Anyway, and Who Decided?

> *I mean, it's easy to romanticize the past. "Oh, we had stellar students." You know, we have stellar students every year, and we have kids who are not doing as well. But our students are not as resilient as they used to be. And I think that's just, like, across the board [from] everything I've read—anxiety, depression, so many of those things on the rise. And I think some of that is that we can identify those students a lot earlier and it's—we don't just chalk it up to ads, teenage moodiness ... yeah, [we know] this person really has a problem.*
>
> Dr. Wilson, Educator

> *I think there's something to be said for the whole adaptability thing too.*
>
> Mrs. Powell, Educator

Girls in the 6th grade class at St. Bernadette Catholic School experienced challenges common to girls around the world, including adversities based on their gender identity and expression, race, social class, sexual orientation, and other areas of social identity. While girls are certainly impacted by these experiences, they are not defined by them. Girls navigate these forms of oppression and find pathways to wellness, strength, healing and resilience. In this chapter, we describe the development of the construct of resilience within the psychological literature and examine how it has been applied within school settings. We delineate some limitations of this construct, particularly the emphasis on individualism. As McRobbie (2020) describes, "Because they are so widely in circulation, we find ourselves taking up these vocabularies [of resilience] and using them, even as we doubt or refute them" (p. 63). We simultaneously recognize that girls often experience educational spaces as adverse and oppressive, and that girls can be resilient in the face of this. Toward that, we offer ways of conceptualizing resilience to focus on processes over outcomes dictated by dominant groups as indicating "success".

DOI: 10.4324/9781003111535-2

What is Resilience?

Within the psychology literature, resilience is often described as "a process or phenomenon reflecting positive child adjustment despite conditions of risk" (Luthar, Lyman, and Crossman, 2014, p. 125). Early resilience work (Garmezy, 1974; Rutter, 1979) identified children who were adapting well despite having parents with severe forms of psychopathology. Werner's work looking at a birth cohort in Kauai described protective factors that helped "at-risk" children achieve positive outcomes (Werner, 1989). During the 1980s and 1990s, these researchers helped to identify sources of resilience, including factors internal to the child and external factors in the family and community. In addition to broadening the scope of sources of resilience, researchers also recognized that resilience is dynamic in terms of changing over time and domain-specific. This means that children can seem "fine" in terms of their external behaviors but might still be struggling internally (Luthar et al., 2014).

Adversity and (positive) adaptation are the two constructs often identified to measure resilience. Rutter (1979) demonstrated that multiple layers of risk (community violence, parental psychopathology, poverty) contributed to significantly increased risk for negative outcomes versus experience of singular risk factors. Positive adaptation can look and be described differently according to the child's developmental stage and the degree of risk, trauma, and adversity. Resilience to a major trauma can be defined as absence of psychopathology, and resilience within a toddler looks different (relationship with caregiver) than resilience within an adolescent (school and social competence). "If studies are truly to be informative to interventions, they must move beyond simply identifying variables linked with competence toward understanding the specific underlying mechanisms" (Luthar et al., 2014, p. 128). One struggle with how resilience research has been presented and understood has to do with confusion about constructs of resilience vs. *ego* resilience. The latter focuses on trait-based personality factors that do not take into account the systems, relationships, and processes that help to promote or prohibit resilience. While researchers have summarized the influential role that parents, peers, educators, mentors, and community (neighborhoods, churches) can play in promoting resilience or intensifying vulnerability (Luthar et al., 2014), there is little mention of the larger role that more distal systems (political systems, media messages, and stereotypes and biases related to social identities) play in risk and resilience.

Explicitly considering definitions of resilience from a variety of disciplines, Southwick et al. (2014) point out that while defining resilience—the ability to withstand, overcome, and become stronger after adversity—is important and useful, it does not accurately capture the complexity of resilience. The interactions among a variety of biopsychosocial factors (including culture and the environment) provide a much more thorough understanding of resilience. Yehuda defines resilience as continuing to move forward, in an integrated way, after experiencing trauma or adversity regardless of whether a mental health diagnosis is included (Southwick et al., 2014). Masten describes the evolution in her thinking of resilience as she has worked with families, communities, and colleagues from different disciplines. She supports a definition that depicts resilience in a more systemic fashion: "the capacity of a dynamic system to adapt successfully to disturbances that threaten the viability, the function, or the development of that system" (Southwick et al., p. 4). Recently, Masten and Motti-Stefanidi (2020) wrote about the importance of understanding resilience as being integrated into the multisystemic spheres that make up children's lives, including families, schools, and communities.

Programs to Promote Resilience

Similar to the way resilience was initially understood from an individual perspective, many efforts to promote resilience have also targeted individuals. A concrete example is the REAL Girls program developed by Mann (2015). "REAL Girls was designed to help struggling middle school girls develop resiliency—particularly academic self-efficacy, school connectedness, and identity—and achieve successful outcomes in school and life" (p. 117). Though the intentions of this work are clearly valuable and important, the program for developing resilience rests squarely on the shoulders of the girls; however, this neither brings awareness to, nor contributes to the dismantling of the barriers to resilience that currently (and historically) exist in the systems girls inhabit. Further, although programs like REAL Girls acknowledge the systems which contribute to girls' stress, discrimination, and harassment, the attempts to promote resilience are exclusively located within individual girls. To be fair, the researcher who developed the program was drawing from and committed to work that promotes characteristics of resilience in girls; the work intentionally focused on internal characteristics of individuals. And the program does seem to offer a great deal of support, including mentoring, discussions of challenges girls face, coping strategies, and examples of adaptive coping and flourishing in the face of adversity. Effectiveness research indicates that the program is successful in promoting the positive outcomes it was designed to impact.

In contrast, based on the model of community resilience (resilience in the face of disaster-based trauma), the GIRRL Power program used Participatory Action Research to support adolescent girls in identifying risk-reduction strategies in their South African community. This community faced multiple levels of health and safety risks to which adolescent girls were found to be particularly vulnerable (Forbes-Genade and Van Niekerk, 2019). The phases of the program included training, reflection, and action for community stakeholders as well as the participants (the girls themselves). The action plan created by the girls involved a community awareness component in addition to community action activities, including collaboration with the public safety department and peer-led activities. It is important to note the role the girls played in the process–their collaboration with community leaders and the recognition of the girls' voices were crucial elements to the success of this program.

Oppression as Adversity

Throughout this book, we examine particular ways misogyny, sexism, and intersecting forms of oppression (racism, classism, and homophobia in particular) function within schools to create adversities to which girls (and educators who work with girls) respond. We situate our work within the body of research seeking to understand girls' and women's experiences of misogyny and sexism. Lott (1995) defines sexism as "the oppression or inhibition of women through a vast network of everyday practices, attitudes, assumptions, behaviors and institutional rules" which can manifest through events on a continuum of severity, including interpersonal discrimination, harassment, and sexual violence (p. 113). Numerous scholars have categorized experiences of interpersonal sexism as often fitting into one of three categories: 1) expectations related to traditional gender role stereotypes, 2) sexual objectification, and 3) demeaning or derogatory comments and behaviors (Brinkman and Rickard, 2009; Kaiser and Miller, 2004; Swim et al., 2001).

Manne (2020) argues that sexism and misogyny are related constructs but offers important distinctions between them. She describes misogyny as the "law enforcement" branch of patriarchy, in which girls and women disproportionately face hostile treatment designed to enforce gender norms and expectations. Girls and women can experience misogyny even without an apparent perpetrator or when the actor thinks he or she does not hold sexist beliefs. Misogynistic hostility can include anything that serves to punish or deter girls and women from actual or perceived challenges to patriarchal expectations and norms (Manne, 2017). This hostility can manifest in the form of ridiculing, shaming, sexualizing or desexualizing girls and women, silencing, and many other types of dismissive behaviors—many of which we document throughout this book.

In our interviews with educators and youth, we asked about girls' experiences of oppression related to their gender identity, social class, race and ethnicity, and sexual orientation. Girls and educators described occurrences of interpersonal sexism, sexism embedded in school climates in the form of policies and procedures, and ways that sexism in the broader culture impacts girls' experiences within schools. Our data reflect how girls experience oppression across what Collins (2002) describes as a matrix of domination. Four interrelated domains of power impact people's lived experiences related to their social identities. These domains include the structural (institutional structures), disciplinary (organizational practices), hegemonic (cultural beliefs and stereotypes), and interpersonal.

Girls' Experiences of Sexism

Girls and young women are subjected to a number of different types of sexism, including blatant, covert, and subtle forms of sexism, which all have harmful impacts on their mental health (Benokraitis, 1997; Dovidio, Glick, and Budman, 2005; Leaper and Brown, 2008). Research suggests that a decrease in self-esteem among adolescent girls can be directly linked to experiences of sexism (Benokraitis, 1997; Kaiser and Miller, 2004). Young women are often treated like they have less worth than their male counterparts, and after some time they might begin to believe it. They also face many constraints and limitations which prevent them from developing a belief that they can exert control over their world. Both of these outcomes of sexism have direct effects on young women's development of self-esteem.

In the data we collected, girls described many forms of interpersonal sexism, including being excluded, teased, called derogatory names, and being pressured to conform to stereotypical gender roles. Experiences of sexual harassment in school, street harassment, sexual objectification, and sexual violence were disturbingly pervasive in our data collected over a decade of time. Sexism was evident in the school climate in several ways, including sexualized dress codes and other forms of sexual objectification, prioritizing of boys over girls (particularly boys' sports), reinforcing stereotypical and toxic masculinity, holding more space in the classroom for boys than girls, and sexism occurring amongst the educators in the school. Girls and educators also described how sexism within the larger society and culture impacted what was happening in the school. Cultural narratives about "locker room talk," victim-blaming, and "boys will be boys" attitudes were often treated as problems outside the school's domain.

We will describe girls' and educators' reports about misogyny and sexism throughout the book as we explore different topics. It is not our intention to provide a comprehensive list of the forms of sexism that girls experience generally or the frequency with which they experience it. Instead, our purpose is to explore how girls and educators make sense of these experiences, what it means to be resilient despite oppression, what resistance looks like, and to explore pathways for educational transformation.

Unequal Treatment in the Classroom

Girls in both phases of our project shared stories of unequal treatment in the classroom. Many girls in the middle school talked about educators who consistently called on the boys more often than girls, even when girls were first to raise their hands. When we asked why they thought this happened, some of the girls blamed themselves. They said that they did not raise their hands often enough or they didn't know the answers. Some of the girls blamed the boys for this, saying that the boys were rowdy and spoke out in class, so the educators called on them more.

INTERVIEWER: Do some members of your class get called on more often than others?

ALYSSA (7TH GRADE): Yeah. Especially in some classes. Two classes of mine. Mostly the boys just take over. And so, they always get called on or whatever.

INTERVIEWER: What happens when you know an answer to a question or you have, like, a really good idea about something that you're talking about in class?

ALYSSA: Usually, of course, the boys are always heard cause they're so loud and they don't raise their hand or anything. They're just, like, opened. They just talk whenever they want to, and so, it's really, really frustrating when, like, girls like us are, like—I can tell the girls too are always raising their hands or sitting in their seats waiting to be heard. And then, like, you don't because, like, everyone else is making fun of you. But they just, like, make fun right in front of you—it doesn't matter.

INTERVIEWER: So, you find that girls try to raise their hand and wait their turn to make a comment?

ALYSSA: Yeah. We try to be more mature and [you] try to get your idea out. And other people are staring at you and then there's chaos, and they just want to quit, like, whatever we were talking about. And you are just like, "Well, I had a good idea."

INTERVIEWER: And it sounds like you're saying that they tend to be in front of you, like physically from where you physically sit. Boys in the front, and the girls sit in the back.

ALYSSA: Like, whenever we have a discussion, one person gets out of their seat and ... then another, right in front of the teacher, like, right where the teacher is, so it's like a complete huddle, and you're just like—all the girls are seating in their seat [going], "Hello? I'm raising my hand."

INTERVIEWER: So, they actually get out of their chair? Get more attention and—

ALYSSA: Yeah. And get closer to the teacher.

The dynamics that Alyssa described are not new or unique to her school. Numerous educational scholars have depicted how schools create and reinforce classroom dynamics that are unfair to girls (Sadker and Sadker, 1994; Sadker and Zittleman, 2009). Several scholars have articulated how post-feminist proclamations and claims about a "boy crisis" in education have shifted conversations away from concerns about unfair treatment of girls in schools (Pomerantz et al., 2013). Data from our follow-up study indicate that classroom dynamics continue to silence girls in order to address boys' "need" for more attention from educators. What we heard from both students and educators are the ways girls are being taught to behave that help educators manage the boys in the classroom.

One high school teacher talked about how he feels that girls in his class are quiet and that he wants them to speak up more.

MR. BAKER: Well, yeah, 'cause... there's more class time devoted to those guys and what they're doing, you know, than there is—and I don't know how we could change this, but then ... there is like, "Okay, now everybody that really has something to say is going to say it. We're going to listen." Um, yeah. I don't know, maybe that has something to do with the class sizes here or something like that.

INTERVIEWER: So, the time spent managing some of the boys' behavior—it's hard to have space for the girls.

MR. BAKER: I put so much energy into that ... and I can imagine that the girls ... I know this for fact because it's a—I think a lot of the girls are, are maybe frustrated that there's not ... enough space for them, you know, because they are at a different level developmentally. I think I feel comfortable saying that. Yeah ... there are the exceptional guys that are like that too at that stage. But I think overall, you're spending most of your energy managing the, you know, the guys and what they're doing and what they're trying to get away with in ninth grade. I don't know. Maybe, maybe once I'm a better teacher that'll, that'll stop. But ... this year ... that's been, that's been an issue.

Mr. Baker expressed frustration with the boys' behavior (speaking over the girls, dominating the space) and said, "I don't know how we could change this," indicating a perception that the boys' behavior is inevitable. He articulated a desire for the girls to speak up more in his classroom but presented the dilemma as being attributable to factors other than misogyny and male entitlement. He ponders whether the problem is large class sizes or girls being more "developmentally mature" than the boys. (We explore this theme of expecting girls to be mature in more detail in Chapter 2.) He was even willing to take ownership of the problem as a teacher—saying that he might better manage the boys when he is a "better teacher." While he might learn some classroom management techniques to address the boys' behavior, it is unfair to expect any one teacher to counteract all the messages the boys receive in this school and society that they are entitled to take up all the space in a room and speak over girls.

Oppression and Intersectionality

We are particularly interested in understanding girls' experiences of oppression related to gender; however, it is essential to scrutinize oppression from an intersectional lens. Intersectionality theory provides a framework for exploring how social identities interact, and examining systems of power, privilege and oppression (Collins, 2015; Brinkman and Donohue, 2020; Cole, 2009; Crenshaw, 1991). We explicitly asked girls and educators about experiences of oppression or inequity related to social class, ethnicity, and sexual orientation. Not surprisingly, both studies included participants who denied that their schools had any indicators of racism, classism, or homophobia. Others spoke in detail about how these aspects of social identity shape students' experiences in school.

Social Class

At Our Lady of Guadalupe Catholic High School, most girls and educators talked extensively about the impact of social class within the school and the stratification of students into different social groups. Despite wearing uniforms—which were described as being intended to "level the playing field"—wealthy students found ways to signal their social class through the types of cars they drove, discussions of their family vacations, or how they spent money (often throwing parties in their parents' homes). Students also described their perception that wealthier students were more popular among their peers and had more power in the school—they were given more voice to change how the school functioned and were granted leeway when they broke the rules. At Our Lady of Guadalupe, the experience of adversity related to social class was framed as a relationship to *not being* one of the wealthy students and not having the associated privileges rather than the treatment of students from less wealthy families. Isabel (12th grade) described her experience with this dynamic:

> I think this is a very—being a private Catholic school, it's a very money-controlled school. Like, there are people who are benefactors. There are people with their names on things who can get away with more things than people who don't.

Conversations about social class and race and ethnicity were often interwoven, which was not surprising, as social class and ethnicity are deeply connected, particularly within the United States. Access to wealth and the resources that build wealth are unequally distributed among White families versus Black and Indigenous families and families of people of color (BIPOC). Data from the 2019 Survey of Consumer Finances revealed ongoing wealth disparities within the United States. According to this data, White families have on average eight times the wealth of Black families and five times the wealth of Latino families (Bhutta et al., 2020). One of the barriers identified for BIPOC students was related to access to material resources. For example, after being asked about potential differences in the school based on students' race or ethnicity, one educator talked about how the school addresses the needs of students who do not have access to the internet at home.

Race and Ethnicity

The experiences of adversity that girls faced based on their race and ethnicity took numerous forms. Color-blind racial ideology—the assertion that one does not see skin color or differences based on race—was articulated by some students and staff members. Neville et al. (2016) define color-blind racial ideology (CBRI) as "the widely held belief that skin color does not play a role in interpersonal interactions and institutional policies/ practices" (p. 5). CBRI consists of two domains: color-evasion and power-evasion (Neville et al., 2013). Color-evasion includes denying racial differences between groups by emphasizing sameness, while power-evasion is the denial of racism by asserting that all groups have equal opportunities. When asked about whether girls have different experiences in the school based on their racial identity, one educator articulated the colorblind ideology. Mrs. Carter said:

> I've watched as society has become a lot more accepting to what I already had developed in my own mind as "you can be anything you want to be—just do what you know is best." You know, it's not a gay or straight, it's not a girl or boy, it's not a black or white issue. It's "Be the best you can be, and do what you know you can do."

Many individuals assert that color-blind racial ideology is a good thing, but denying race and ignoring racism causes harm because it perpetuates myths about equal opportunities and blames people of color for the adverse outcomes they experience (Neville et al., 2016). Color-blind racial ideology can be particularly harmful to students when it is endorsed by educators and administrators in K-12 schools. Educators might believe that it will result in fair practices and decisions if they ignore race and racism. Instead, the common outcome is ignoring the beliefs, policies, and structures that discriminate against students of color (Castro-Atwater, 2016). When educators avoid discussions about race and emphasize "sameness" among students, they prevent essential opportunities to develop critical thinking about race and trivialize discrimination experienced by students of color (2016).

> "When people claim they don't see race, it often means they don't see those who are assumed to bring race with them (white: not of color; race: of color). 'I don't see race' thus translates as: I don't see those who are not white as not white, which translates as: I don't see not white. In order not to disappear, you have to make your brownness willful. Again: Some have to become willful just to appear."
>
> (Ahmed, 2016, p. 119)

Educators and girls described what they perceived to be students' self-segregation—students tended to spend time in groups based on their racial identity. Participants generally presented self-segregation as a non-problematic dynamic that the students chose. Tatum (2017) offers a nuanced understanding of the racial dynamics playing out inside (and outside) schools that influence how children and adolescents socialize within schools. Many of our conversations that began with the assertion of self-segregation turned into discussions about some students being marginalized and less visible within the school. Students and educators utilized two different terms to describe the groups of students who were often on the fringes of the school, based on their race or ethnicity—"English as a second language (ESL) learners" and "international students." Although many students technically fit both of these terms—they were used to refer to different groups of students. The term "international student" was most often used to refer to students from East Asian countries who attended the school as part of an exchange program. In contrast, the term "ESL learner" was most often used to refer to students whose first language was Spanish and who were first- or second-generation immigrants from Central or South America. The international students were described as being isolated and unknown by most of the other students in the school, but generally, this was treated as unproblematic and perhaps by choice of the students themselves.

Students and staff members also described incidents of hostile and blatant racism within their schools. Mr. Walker shared an incident that shocked him when asked about how he responds to girls' reports of sexism: "The one thing that I went straight to the counselor myself for was he [a coach] was telling me that he played a game, 'Whites versus the world.'" Students and educators talked about racism impacting Latinx students at Our Lady of Guadalupe Catholic High School. Some girls shared that they felt educators had lower expectations of them because they identify as Latina, and they were not given the same opportunities to excel. Girls also talked about racial microaggressions and dynamics with their peers. Maria (12th grade) shared:

> I'm kind of, like, more white-passing, so … they sort of, like, they forget that that's a thing. Like, one time, someone said something racist, and I called them out for it, and he was like, "Why are you offended? I don't even consider you Mexican."

Some of the racism targeting Latinx population was explicit and hostile, including disparaging comments about immigration and immigrants.

Sexual Orientation and Gender Identity

Students depicted experiences of oppression related to sexual orientation and gender identity. While we as authors note that there are important distinctions between these categories of identity, students often spoke about them together. One of the areas where we saw the most significant and most explicit change over time was the increased acceptance of LGBTQIA+ identified students. However, this trend was not universal or without complications. Other scholars have noted similar changes in attitudes about gender identity and sexual orientation, perhaps more among youth than educators, during the time spanning from our first study to the second one. One study collected data from 305 pre-kindergarten through 12th-grade educators in the United States from 2006 until 2014 (Hall and Rodgers, 2019). They found that in general, teacher's attitudes about homosexuality have become more favorable over time, although some still hold negative stereotypes.

In the first phase of our study, a student in the 6th grade shared that her peers sometimes called her "gay" or "lesbian" as a slur when they fought with her or teased her. We did not hear about this type of harassment in our second study (which does not mean it was entirely absent from the school). We suspect that this type of harassment was less frequent both at the high school level (compared to middle school) and resulted from changing attitudes and intentional efforts to get students to stop using these terms in a derogatory way. Within the United States, there have been widespread efforts to raise awareness about the impact of derogatory language. Scholars have described how use of this language is harmful to LGBTQIA students. Even when the language is subtle or not directly targeted at a student who identifies as LGBTQIA, these terms are a form of microaggressions—common interactions that happen in one's daily life. The impact of microaggressions can accumulate and is associated with feelings of victimization, suicidal thinking, and higher rates of substance abuse, depression, and other health problems for LGBTQIA students (Nadal, 2013).

In 2010 girls described the atmosphere in their high school as having a reluctant acceptance of girls who identified as lesbian or were romantically involved with other girls, but less acceptance of boys who identified as gay. Lisa (11th grade) said:

> I mean, at first, people are like, "She's dating a girl." And, like, we haven't seen—I don't think we've seen boys actually dating each other, but we've seen girls so ... And at first, everybody is like, "I didn't know she was." And so, it's kinda weird at the beginning, and then it just goes away. You get used to it."

In general, the school climate at Christ the King High School in 2010 was described as being not openly hostile to gay or lesbian students. Sloan (11th grade) shared,

> Yeah, I think so because—I don't know. I think that our school is pretty non-judgmental, like, we don't beat up the kids for being gay. I think it would better be, like, than hiding it because some people would be like, "Oh, I know you are gay. You're denying it."

Students participating in the follow-up study in 2016 generally agreed that at Our Lady of Guadalupe, the school climate was one of tolerance for students who identified as LGBTQIA. However, there were questions raised about the difference between tolerance and inclusion. Some students indicated that those students who didn't identify as cisgender or heterosexual were often invisible in the school, and efforts to increase visibility or celebrate these students' identities were often suppressed. For example, administrators told students who attempted to form a gay-straight alliance in the school that they could not do so. The school climate reflected what we termed "rainbow blindness"—attitudes suggesting one does not "see" gender identity or sexual orientation, that it should be ignored so as not to make a big deal about it.

Longing for Resilience

The term *resilience* rarely came up in our interviews with girls or educators, but at times, there was a narrative that reflected some of the traditional ways resilience has been understood in the psychological literature. Very often, educators turned to this narrative as something that was missing, as something that girls need, and/or as something that girls used to have in a prior era. The resilience narrative often included recognition of some challenge or adversity that girls were facing and a way that girls could better cope with the hardship to experience less distress. At times, the resilience narrative functioned to make the initial adversity non-existent—that the experience is not the problem, but rather the problem is the girl's inability to cope with it. Sometimes a resilience narrative was interwoven with post-feminist arguments that external conditions for boys and girls are equal; therefore, if girls are struggling, the problem is with their lack of ability to deal with stressors.

INTERVIEWER: Thinking back on this school year, have there been any situations where you felt like students were treated differently because they are female? Or were students reporting to you that their perception was something was different because they're a girl?

MRS. CARTER: So, the answer to the question, bottom line, is, yes. But I'm not sure that it's so much related to stereotyping or judging based on female versus male as it is their inabilities to, at this point in time, have a lot of coping skills.

This use of resilience as coping with adversity was also taken up at times by educators with a nostalgic tone. As we see in the opening quote for this chapter, some of the discussions of resilience implied that girls (and all youth) used to be more resilient than they are now. Some of the conversations indicated a sense of loss of ability on girls' parts to deal with stressful situations. Ms. Brown said:

> Like, acknowledging at least after all this time that okay, I can understand that there are pressures, not everybody's equipped to handle them. I think we've gotten our kids less good at handling them because we over-manage them so much … that they don't have a chance to work a lot of stuff out on their own.

Sometimes, an educator described their recognition that a system is unfair or biased but saw resilience as the pathway to growth or wellness for girls. Ms. Brown commented, "So yeah, my whole thing is just, like, yeah … there's a system in place, doesn't mean it's perfect, and we can always tweak it. But, you know, learn to work it from within." We understand this use of a resilience narrative to be rooted in wanting what is best for girls and seeing oneself as realistic and honest with girls. We also read this use of the narrative as tied to learned helplessness—a sense that the systems we live in will not improve, so our best option is to work hard to succeed within them. We explore these narratives and their impact on girls in Chapter 3.

If Not Resilience, Then What?

Clonan-Roy, Jacobs, and Nakkula (2016) describe resilience as a competency because, "it is unavoidable that adolescent girls of color will experience situations of adversity (including challenges related to racism, classism, and gender- and ethnic- discrimination) and therefore need to develop attitudes and behaviors that prevent them from internalizing these experiences" (p. 114). This view of resilience stresses that girls need to develop the competency of resilience because there is oppression, harassment, and racism in the larger social, cultural, and contextual systems, *not* a problem or deficit in individual girls. Further, Clonan-Roy et al. (2016) emphasize the dynamic rather than static nature of resilience, so that "adult allies should recognize girls' actions, beliefs, and statements that represent emerging and maturing resilient processes and nurture them accordingly" (p.114). Finally, the authors suggest that researchers need to take a longer view of resilience that considers contextual factors, intersecting identities, and the political systems in which girls live.

Ungar (2012, 2015, 2018) has written extensively on what he refers to as "social ecologies" and resilience. To understand resilience, we must look at the individual in relation to their social and physical environments, and it is the interaction between individual and environment plus context where we see resilience. Understanding resilience as multisystemic allows for interventions and support for parents and educators who then contribute to improved well-being and resilience for children (Twum-Antwi, Jefferies, and Ungar 2020). Throughout this book, we attempt to look at the dynamic, nuanced, and resistance-oriented ways girls talk about resilience. We seek to understand how the larger educational system has provided and/or failed to provide support and resources for educators and students that contribute to healthy and adaptive development for all.

References

Ahmed, S. (2016). *Living a feminist life*. Duke University Press.

Benokraitis, N. (Ed.) (1997) *Subtle Sexism: Current Practice and Prospects forChange*. Thousand Oaks: Sage Publications.

Bhutta, N., Chang, A.C., Dettling, L.J., and Hsu, J.W. (2020). *Disparities in Wealth by Race and Ethnicity in the 2019 Survey of Consumer Finances*. Board of Governors of the Federal Reserve System. doi:10.17016/2380-7172.2797.

Brinkman, B.G. and Donohue, P (2020). Doing intersectionality in social justice oriented clinical training. *Training and Education in Professional Psychology, 14*(2), 109–115. doi:10.1037/tep0000274.

Brinkman, B.G. and Rickard, K.M. (2009). College students' descriptions of everyday gender prejudice. *Sex Roles*, 61(7–8), 461–475. doi:10.1007/s11199-009-9643-3.

Castro-Atwater, S.A. (2016). Color-blind racial ideology in K-12 schools. In H.A. Neville, M.E. Gallardo, and D.W. Sue (Eds). *The myth of racial color blindness: Manifestations, dynamics, and impact* (pp. 207–226). American Psychological Association. doi:10.1037/14754-000.

Clonan-Roy, K., Jacobs, C.E., and Nakkula, M.J. (2016). Towards a model of positive youth development specific to girls of color: Perspectives on development, resilience, and empowerment. *Gender Issues*, 33(2), 96–121. doi:10.1007/s12147-016-9156-7.

Cole, E.R. (2009). Intersectionality and research in psychology. *American Psychologist*, 64, 170–180. doi:10.1037/a0014564.

Collins, P.H. (2015). Intersectionality's definitional dilemmas. *Annual Review of Sociology*, 41, 1–20. http://dx.doi.org/10.1146/annurev-soc073014-112142.

Collins, P.H. and Bilge, S. (2016). *Intersectionality*. Polity Press.

Crenshaw, K. (1991). Mapping the margins: Intersectionality, identity politics, and violence against women of color. *Stanford Law Review*, 43, 1241–1299. doi:10.2307/1229039.

Dovidio, J.F., Glick, P., and Rudman, L.A. (Eds). (2008). *On the nature of prejudice: Fifty years after Allport*. John Wiley & Sons.

Forbes-Genade, K. and Van Niekerk, D. (2019). GIRRL power! Participatory Action Research for building girl-led community resilience in South Africa. *Action Research*, 17(2), 237–257. doi:10.1177/1476750318756492.

Garmezy, N. (1974). The study of competence in children at risk for severe psychopathology. In E.J. Anthony and C. Koupernik (Eds), *The child in his family: Vol. 3: Children at psychiatric risk* (pp. 77–97). Wiley.

Hall, W.J. and Rodgers, G.K. (2019). Teachers' attitudes toward homosexuality and the lesbian, gay, bisexual, and queer community in the United States. *Social Psychology of Education*, 22(1), 23–41. doi:10.1007/s11218-018-9463-9.

Kaiser, C.R. and Miller, C.T. (2004). A stress and coping perspective on confronting sexism. *Psychology of Women Quarterly*, 28(2), 168–178. doi:10.1111/j.1471-6402.2004.00133.x.

Leaper, C. and Brown, C. S. (2008). Perceived experiences with sexism among adolescent girls. *Child development*, 79(3), 685–704.

Lott, B. (1995). Distancing from women: interpersonal sexist discrimination. In Lott, B. and D. Maluso (Eds), *The social psychology of interpersonal discrimination* (pp. 12–49). Guilford Press.

Luthar S.S., Lyman, E.L., and Crossman, E.J. (2014). Resilience and positive psychology. In *Handbook of developmental psychopathology* (pp. 125–140). Springer US. https://doi.org/10.1007/978-1-4614-9608-3_7.

Manne, K. (2017). *Down girl: The logic of misogyny.* Oxford University Press.

Manne, K. (2020). *Entitled: How male privilege hurts women.* The Crown Publishing Group.

Mann, M.J., Smith, M.L., and Kristjansson, A.L. (2015). Improving academic self-efficacy, school connectedness, and identity in struggling middle school girls: A preliminary study of the REAL Girls program. *Health Education & Behavior*, 42 (1), 117–126. doi:10.1177/1090198114543005.

Masten, A. S. and Motti-Stefanidi, F. (2020). Multisystem resilience for children and youth in disaster: Reflections in the context of COVID-19. *Adversity and Resilience Science*, 1(2), 95–106. https://link.springer.com/article/10.1007/s42844-020-00010-w.

McRobbie, A. (2020). *Feminism and the politics of resilience: Essays on gender, media and the end of welfare.* John Wiley & Sons.

Nadal, K.L. (2013). *That's so gay!: Microaggressions and the lesbian, gay, bisexual, and transgender community.* American Psychological Association.

Neville, H.A., Awad, G.H., Brooks, J.E., Flores, M.P., and Bluemel, J. (2013). Color-blind racial ideology: Theory, training, and measurement implications in psychology. *American Psychologist*, 68(6), 455. www.doi.org/10.1037/a0033282.

Neville, H.A., Gallardo, M.E., and Sue, D.W. (Eds). (2016). Introduction: Has the United States really moved beyond race? In H.A. Neville, M.E. Gallardo, and D. W. Sue (Eds), *The myth of racial color blindness: Manifestations, dynamics, and impact* (pp. 3–21). American Psychological Association. doi:10.1037/14754-001.

Pomerantz, S., Raby, R., and Stefanik, A. (2013). Girls run the world?: Caught between sexism and postfeminism in school. *Gender and Society*, 27(2), 185–207. doi:10.1177/0891243212473199.

Rutter, M. (1979). Protective factors in children's responses to stress and disadvantage. In M.W. Kent and J.E. Rolf (Eds), *Primary prevention in psychopathology, Vol. 3: Social competence in children* (pp. 49–74). University Press of New England.

Sadker, M. and Sadker, D. (1994). *Failing at fairness: How America's schools cheat girls.* Scribners.

Sadker, D. and Zittleman, K.R. (2009). *Still failing at fairness: How gender bias cheats girls and boys in school and what we can do about it.* Simon & Schuster.

Southwick, S.M., Bonanno, G.A., Masten, A.S., Panter-Brick, C., and Yehuda, R. (2014). Resilience definitions, theory, and challenges: Interdisciplinary perspectives. *European Journal of Psychotraumatology*, 5(1). doi:10.3402/ejpt.v5.25338.

Swim, J.K., Hyers, L.L., Cohen, L.L., and Ferguson, M.J. (2001). Everyday sexism: Evidence for its incidence, nature, and psychological impact from three daily diary studies. *Journal of Social Issues*, 57(1), 31–53. doi:10.1111/0022-4537.00200.

Tatum, B.D. (2017). *Why are all the Black kids sitting together in the cafeteria? And other conversations about race.* Basic Books.

Twum-Antwi, A., Jefferies, P., and Ungar, M. (2020). Promoting child and youth resilience by strengthening home and school environments: A literature review. *International Journal of School & Educational Psychology*, 8(2), 78–89. doi:10.1080/21683603.2019.1660284.

Ungar, M. (2012). Social ecologies and their contribution to resilience. In M. Ungar (Ed.), *The social ecology of resilience: A handbook of theory and practice* (pp. 13–31). Springer Science + Business Media. https://doi.org/10.1007/978-1-4614-0586-3_2.

Ungar, M. (2015). Practitioner review: Diagnosing childhood resilience–A systemic approach to the diagnosis of adaptation in adverse social and physical ecologies. *Journal of Child Psychology and Psychiatry*, 56(1), 4–17. https://doi.org/10.1111/jcpp.12306.

Ungar, M. (2018). Systemic resilience. *Ecology and Society*, 23(4). www.jstor.org/stable/26796886.

Werner, E.E. (1989). Children of the Garden Island. *Scientific American*, 260(4), 106–111. www.jstor.org/stable/10.2307/24987220.

Chapter 2

Good Girls, Smart Girls, and Super Girls

OLIVIA (12TH GRADE): *So, the school kind of does a Guadalupe boy and Guadalupe girl thing, and it's an award that's given out at the end of the year for the seniors. I think that basically the male standard is just doing sports and have a pretty [good] grade point average of 3.0. And the girls, they are expected to do so much more and be involved in all these extracurriculars and also have a really high GPA and also be super attractive and well known and popular kind of thing.*

INTERVIEWER: *So, girls have to do it all...*

OLIVIA: *It's like the ultimate multi-tasker. It's crazy.*

Each year at graduation, Our Lady of Guadalupe Catholic High School presents one male and one female "outstanding" student award. In addition to the explicit exclusion of students who identify as gender non-binary or transgender, the annual contest reveals a disturbing pattern of differential expectations for boys compared to girls. In particular, the award embodies adults' unrealistic expectations for girls' success. Members of the administration select the student winners, (neglecting faculty input), thereby demonstrating their perceptions of achievement among students. Consistently at Our Lady of Guadalupe, the "Boy of the Year" is immersed in sports (often more than one), but might or might *not* be a student government leader nor at the top of the class. He is the epitome of hegemonic masculinity. In contrast, the "Girl of the Year" is expected to be academically strong, live up to a particular moral code, be involved in school activities, *and* be traditionally attractive and popular. She is what we refer to as a "Super Girl," a title for one of three interrelated narratives we describe in this chapter that are frequently deemed indicators of resilience among girls. The other two are the "Good Girl" and the "Smart Girl."

The Good Girl type manifests when girls follow the rules, are emotionally mature, and are sexually naive/innocent. The Smart Girl label emerges from adults' expectations that girls should succeed in school. The Super Girl excels in multiple ways—she is academically successful while also being socially adept and talented in other areas (often sports or arts), all while

DOI: 10.4324/9781003111535-3

being deemed physically attractive. The expectations of all three are constructed based on stereotypes of gender, social class, and ethnicity. These three ways of being have been explored in the literature about girls' experiences in (and outside of) school. We describe how these roles revealed themselves in our data and how we make sense of them within the resilience framework.

These three constructs are not static identities but rather ideas put upon and/or taken up by girls intentionally, strategically, or subconsciously. These ways of being offer girls avenues for navigating patriarchal systems and contradictory and unjust expectations and treatment. Multiple forces—internal and external to the girls—construct these identities. They develop through cultural, interpersonal, and intrapsychic discourses. We label the three identities to name how some forces merge into patterns. Yet, we encourage the reader to hold these identities loosely and explore the "possibilities [they open] up for the theorizing of the diverse, conflicting, and disorderly ways in which individuals as subjects identify and/or do not identify with the 'positions' to which they are summoned" (Gonick, 2003; p. 10).

Good Girls

The "Good Girl" stereotype is far from new. Expectations to conform to this ideal—and consequences for challenging it—have sparked feminist movements throughout the world over centuries. Conventional ideals of femininity range from smiling to nurturing to being non-confrontational (Lipkin, 2009). The specific parameters of this standard shift over time, are culturally situated, and intersect with expectations related to multiple demographics. In our work, we describe the Good Girl using three core components: 1) compliance with rules and authority, 2) emotional maturity and caretaking, and 3) modesty (sexual and otherwise). Simmons (2009) describes similar qualities that define the Good Girl based on interviews with middle-class adolescent girls. When asked about the qualities that define Good Girls, they listed traits including being people-pleasers, following the rules, avoiding expressing anger, and not sharing strong opinions.

Good Girls communicate that they trust systems (whether or not they *feel* trust is another story) and support the status quo. In our studies, when asked about inequity or unfairness in their schools, some girls articulated that everything is fair, even as they shared examples suggesting otherwise. At times they justified unequal treatment or problematic decisions made by authority figures. For example, when asked if boys and girls are treated differently in school, Nora (12th grade) said, "I notice that with teachers—little things [like], 'I'll have a group of guys do it' or something. It's little things that they aren't conscious of what they're saying." While she is naming ways that boys and girls are treated differently, she is also excusing this behavior as unintentional on the part of the teachers.

While a feature of being a Good Girl includes following the rules, this does not mean that girls *agree* with the rules. Compliance can be a strategy for navigating unfair systems. Many girls we interviewed described how boys were allowed to break the rules more often than they were—that there was even an expectation that boys would be non-compliant. Grace (12th grade) noted, "I definitely think that this is just like home life, school life, girls are supposed to be perfect, and guys are, well if you mess up, it's ok." Even some educators noted that boys are allowed to break the rules more often than girls are. Mrs. Moore remarked, "The admin will kind of turn the other way and not really acknowledge it when boys are behaving in a more of a bullying kind of way. Girls wouldn't be allowed to do some of the same kinds of things." Good Girls might learn that the consequences for rebellion are too severe. The social capital gained by being seen as compliant by authority figures—including educators—might be a more productive pathway to getting ones' needs met.

Compliance with rules is related to other characteristics of Good Girls, including emotional maturity and caretaking. In our studies, educators shared that they asked girls more questions about their emotions and expected them to be more emotionally mature than boys. For example, Mr. Walker explained that some educators expect girls to be more emotional than boys, and reinforce that stereotype in class, "This teacher in particular, kind of gave that vibe of that girls should be emotional and caring about prayer, boys just be there for the prayer." Educators also often explicitly linked girls' compliance and classroom behavior to emotional maturity—arguing that girls obeyed rules and were less rowdy in the classroom because they were "naturally" more mature than the boys. Another educator, Ms. Powell shared her belief that girls are more mature than boys:

> First of all, because the girls are already intellectually more mature, you know, that age—14 years old. And emotionally, like I said, they're more diplomatic. They're just more sensitive about, you know, how people are maybe going to feel about something, and these poor guys are just kind of clueless.

This language of "maturity" often implied that the differences between girls and boys resulted from a natural (perhaps assumed to be biological?) process in which girls develop faster than boys. Students and educators in our studies are not alone in asserting such expectations that girls are more mature than boys. In her extensive study of discipline in schools, Raby (2012) found many educators stated that they expected girls to be more mature than boys and thus disciplined girls more harshly when they broke the rules. Many educators endorsed stereotypes that boys are more likely to misbehave than girls; some articulated that they punished boys less often, conveying a "boys will be boys" attitude. The framing of girls as *naturally* more mature than boys neglects to recognize that girls are *taught* that maturity and emotional caretaking are expected in order to be a Good Girl. Messages from school, the media, and their family and friends teach girls that they are supposed to be "good" and just what that entails—including assertions to "be nice" to others (Brown, 2003). Therefore, what is described as emotional maturity might be an outcome of being attuned to the school system because girls have learned that this will help them navigate the experiences of oppression they face.

Emotional caretaking shows up in girls' relationships with each other, often in the form of being friendly or kind. Many middle-school girls in our study articulated that the "ideal" girl is nice to others. These girls are not alone in the belief. As Danna Simmons argued we are a "society raising girls to be loving and nice" (2002, p. 7). Good Girls are always expected to show empathy, compassion, and sensitivity to others' needs (Hinshaw and Kranz, 2009). When we dig beneath this surface expectation to be nice, we find the message that to be a Good Girl one should prioritize others' feelings over their own. Good Girls suppress their feelings of anger and avoid conflicts and confrontations. They put the needs of others above their own and avoid setting limits or taking up too much space. Isabell (12th grade) talked about her experiences transferring into the school and trying to demonstrate to the other girls that she was a "nice" girl who would not pose a threat to the existing social dynamics:

> I kind of wanted to tell people I'm not a threat at all, I'm not here to, like, threaten your social hierarchy. I'm here to meet new people because I don't know anyone and I'm two thousand miles from home and I'm just trying to fit in here. But yeah, I just kind of wanted them to know that I'm not here to mess anything up.

This emotional caretaking expectation is particularly salient in relationships with boys—even more so when there is a romantic relationship between a girl and boy. The expectation that Good Girls caretake boys' emotions is part of a culture of misogyny in which girls learn that not taking care of boys' emotional needs can be dangerous and could result in social (and physical) consequences. Such asymmetrical moral support roles are one aspect of misogyny (Manne, 2017). We explore the many ways girls navigate the emotional fragility of boys in detail in Chapter 5.

The third component of the Good Girl is modesty—both sexually and otherwise. The Good Girl is careful not to be too outspoken about her virtues and accomplishments (primarily for fear of making others feel bad). They often downplay their strengths or avoid talking about them. The middle-school girls often struggled to answer the question, "What are things that you like about yourself?" That doesn't mean Good Girls can't or don't excel, but they often do so quietly—even when it gets in the way of their own success. When talking about girls' academic success, Erin (11th grade) said, "You should be modest about it, and stuff like that. So, yeah, I definitely think it prevents us from pushing ourselves and wanting to be the best we can be."

Good Girls are also modest sexually—even to the point of being seen as innocent or naïve about sex and sexuality. One of the quickest ways for a girl to lose status as a Good Girl is to be *perceived* by others as being too sexual (regardless of the girl's actual behavior). Girls often can affirm their own "goodness" regarding sexuality by asserting that the sexual behaviors of other girls are not appropriate (Raby, 2012). Thus, girls work to maintain their status as Good Girls, even if they engage in sexual behavior, by defining others' sexuality as bad. While this expectation might come most often from peers, educators were not free from it. One teacher in our study who celebrated strong, smart, feminist girls also discussed her concerns about girls engaging in sexting behaviors.

It is important to note that all girls do not have equal access to being a Good Girl, as Sharon Lamb (2002) reminds us:

> Because ideals of goodness often are confused with real or possible behavior, living, breathing girls cannot live up to the image and find themselves demoralized from trying. Not only does the ideal shut out girls from the low-income neighborhoods whose lives don't match up, it rejects middle-class girls who know in their heart that they are not as good as they should be.
>
> (p.147)

Black girls, Indigenous girls, and Latina girls are not given the benefit of the doubt afforded to White girls, and their behaviors are less likely to be perceived through the Good Girl lens. In addition to the hidden curriculum in schools that reinforces traditional femininity, schools have adopted more overt and punitive systems to control girls, especially girls of color (Chesney-Lind and Irwin, 2008). According to data gathered by the US Department of Education's Office of Civil Rights, Black girls, Indigenous girls, and Latina girls are more likely to be disciplined in school than their White counterparts. Disproportionate discipline of Black girls is so severe that educational scholar Monique Morris developed the term "pushout" to describe the pressures that are pushing Black girls out of educational systems (Morris, 2016). Numerous scholars have shown that White girls and Black, Indigenous, and Latina girls engage in the same behaviors, but they are interpreted differently by educators. Girls of color are often disciplined for discretionary and subjective offenses, such as "defiance." Instead of being viewed as Good Girls, Black girls are frequently given harsh labels from adults, such as "angry" or "violent." If an adult's mental image of the Good Girl is a White girl, then girls of color will be more often deemed not to measure up and educators will discipline girls accordingly.

Smart Girls

In our study, participants described Smart Girls as doing well in school and viewing academics as an essential path to the future they want for themselves. Compared to the Super Girls, which we describe later in this chapter, Smart Girls are considered less well-rounded and have less social capital. Isabel (12th grade) describes smart girls as not being socially accepted: "I mean, I think a lot of them kind of get belittled a little bit. They're not as popular because they value things other than going to parties and hooking up with guys and being this person." Their primary identity is about academic achievement, and while they are generally compliant with rules, they also use their intellectual power to challenge the rules.

In terms of acceptance and expectations for Smart Girls, educators generally saw the schools as a positive environment for them. Dr. Wilson shared her perspective about the school environment for Smart Girls as being supportive. "I think overall ... there's not a huge problem in being a smart girl.... [W]hen I think about our Salutatorian, Valedictorian, [and] some of the other girls that are really smart girls, I mean, they are well-liked." While educators within this study shared positive perceptions of Smart Girls in the schools, the notion of girls' domination in academic achievement is more controversial outside the classroom. Pomerantz and Raby (2017) urge us to consider the way that the ascension of the Smart Girl is framed against the failure of boys—or the way schools have failed boys—and a "feminization" of schools that has favored girls. Feared outcomes of these disparities includes women gaining greater power and damage to traditional masculinity. The popular press has had numerous pieces depicting postfeminist arguments claiming that girls' academic successes have come at the expense of boys (*Business Week, New York Times, The Nation*, among others). However, Pomerantz and Raby (2017) point out that it is problematic to look from this unidirectional, contextless perspective, obscuring the challenges girls continue to face, despite their seeming dominance in academics.

The girls we interviewed shared that Smart Girls were respected by their peers and the teachers. For example, Olivia (12th grade) commented, "I think they are treated really well. Most of the people like most of the girls in that popular crowd or [girls who are] smart, all in AP classes." Ava (12th grade) noted that her male friends respected girls for being smart:

> I think they [smart girls] are treated with a lot of respect. I think, at least from my guy friends, and—even maybe it's not necessarily a good thing—for me, even when I know that someone else is also smart and they don't sit there and just look pretty, then, like, they get a lot more respect.

Maria (12th grade) shared that younger girls might be less confident about their intelligence, but she sees her peers as supportive:

> I think that educators appreciate smart students, so I think that's good. From students, I don't think there's any stereotype, like, 'Oh, we hate smart kids,' or, like, 'nerds.' ...like, I don't think that exists in our grade, but I'm not sure; that might be a thing for younger [grades], just because that's something [some] kids are insecure about when they're younger.

During our conversations with young women, we came across numerous caveats to the narrative of acceptance of intelligence in girls. They articulated that smartness is valued in girls if they are also pretty, athletic, humble, and not too assertive (thus making them Super Girls, which we describe below). Some girls spoke about social struggles (particularly in relation to boys) of being a Smart Girl. For example, Rebecca (11th grade) shared details of her experience of social isolation as a Smart Girl:

> [Smart girls are] uncool because...or, I think a little of that might just be jealous[y], just because, like, they're not smart ... Well, I think that's how people sometimes view me, but they're like, "Oh, she totally has it figured out, and she wouldn't be interested in coming to parties."

It is possible for girls to be popular and smart; however, for girls who are smart and *not* popular, their intelligence is used as the excuse for not being accepted. It is a challenging and confusing tightrope for girls to navigate. Even if Smart Girls gain acceptance, it is tenuous and based on how they interact with others. Many girls in our study shared that one way they think girls navigate the tightrope of social acceptance is to downplay their intelligence.

MYAH (11TH GRADE): I think actually a lot of the girls are smart, but they'll pretend they're not.

INTERVIEWER: That's part of the next question. So, tell me what you mean by that, or explain that a little.

MYAH: They'll just act dumb but then academically, you're seeing the classes they're taking and you're like, "You're actually pretty smart." But then they basically make these stupid comments, and you're just like, "Why did you just say that?"

INTERVIEWER: So, that's the next question, right. Why do you think they do that?

MYAH: I guess just to try to achieve this kind of acceptance from everyone else in that they're one of them ... It's as if it's not cool to be smart if you're a girl because ... I know they know the answer to those stupid questions. I know they wouldn't ask that on a normal day if they were with other people, but the fact that they're at school with ... people who expect them to act a certain way, they will change their actions and their speech and become this totally different person. And they seem really fake and not true and real to themselves.

Several girls in our studies talked about girls minimizing their intelligence to protect boys' feelings. We explore this experience in Chapter 5 as we describe how girls navigate fragile masculinity.

It is important to note that bias against women concerning intellectual ability persists despite the success women and girls have had at every level of academic achievement. Bian, Leslie, and Cimpian (2018) have experimental evidence of this bias. Children as young as five were, initially, more likely to choose teammates of their own gender for a game proposed by the researchers. However, when the game required players to be "smart," fewer girls were chosen. In addition, Bian, Leslie, and Cimpian (2017) found that girls as young as six years old were less likely to identify women as being "really, really smart" (p. 389). One outcome of such biases is fewer women represented in fields/careers that require "genius" including STEM and fields like philosophy and physics. Further, this gendered bias creates limitations for girls in their self-efficacy, intellectual ability, and areas of passion/interest that are available to them. Moreover, in another series of experiments, adults were less likely to refer to women for employment/career opportunities that required "brilliance," and this was true whether the recommender was a man or a woman (Bian, Leslie, and Cimpian, 2018). Furthermore, Storage et al. (2020) have found evidence of an implicit "gender-brilliance stereotype" whereby people associate brilliance/genius with being male. This was demonstrated via implicit measures and was true for participants across a wide variety of ages around the world. Teachers' differential responses to boys and girls in the classroom is one place where this bias is socialized. When it comes to careers that require "brilliance" or "raw talent," particularly among academics, women are more likely to report feeling like imposters, and this finding is even more likely for those with underrepresented and marginalized identities (Muradoglu et al., 2021).

Pomerantz and Raby (2017) interviewed boys about their experiences being smart and their perceptions of what it is like for Smart Girls. Most boys agreed that it was more challenging for girls to be considered anything other than "smart" and that as long as boys are not perceived as studying too much or trying too hard, they often did *not* experience negative consequences for being smart. While boys might have to navigate being smart in terms of how other *boys* see them, girls face potential social challenges from both boys *and* other girls.

Many questions arise in terms of Smart Girls concerning popularity. The degree of choice or agency that girls express in whether or not they want to be popular is worth consideration. Some girls express curiosity or even concern about lack of popularity, keeping them from Super Girl status. Others speak to a clear choice to focus attention on academics rather than spending time on a social life or the trappings of stereotypical femininity that might (or might not) increase their social status.

Super Girls

The Super Girl is a recent iteration of the unrealistic expectations for girls to achieve perfection. The Super Girl has to *be* it all and *do* it all. She is academically strong and known for being intelligent. However, she differs from the Smart Girl profile in ways that make her intelligence more readily accepted by peers and adults. She is considered "well-rounded" by excelling in at least one area in addition to academics, whether it is athletics or other extracurricular activities. She is often a leader and is confident and motivated. She is socially adept and well-liked (or at least respected) by her peers and adults. She is also conventionally attractive and conforms to expectations of femininity in her style and dress. Most often, the Super Girl is White, middle/upper class, heterosexual, and cisgender.

The Super Girl is the ultimate expression of girl power. She is a celebration of the belief that girls can do and be anything: She reaps the benefits of feminists who have fought for equal opportunities for girls. The Super Girl embodies the "You Go Girl!" feminism that is the focus of most of the feel-good media coverage about girls (Chaudhry, 2007). We introduce the Super Girl in the section about resilience because, much like the Good Girl and Smart Girl, the Super Girl is often read as resilient—that she is thriving in our systems. While we also celebrate girls' strengths, talents, and leadership, we remain concerned that the emphasis on Super Girl's successes mask the challenges she faces, including the immense pressure to be "Super."

During our conversations with girls and educators, we found that questions about how Smart Girls are treated often lead to discussions about the Super Girl. For example, at Our Lady of Guadalupe Catholic High School, one student, Grace (12th grade) explained how smart girls are viewed and treated in her school in detail. She related her experiences and the experience of one of her close friends:

> So, me and my friend—we're really close. But we're also right on that edge for Valedictorian so, yeah. It's like, "What did you get on that test?" [laughter] Like, every point counts. So ... whereas I'm better at certain stuff, she [is] better at other stuff. But she is a genius at math, and I love math, and it bugs me because I'm not as good as her. But she is also so helpful because she helps me, and, like, we're really close that way. But the thing is, I am definitely more of the—I have the sports going for me too. So, because of the sports, and because of my personality and the way I come off, I have always been put in ... If there's a splinter, where there's like, the nerdy, quiet on this side, and the popular on this side, I'm always more towards *that* [popular] side, so I have the guys that like me. The thing is, she is gorgeous as well, and, like, guys are always like, "She is so hot," but she is, like, too nerdy or too smart. I can't do that. But the thing is, I am the exact same way. But

> because I did sports, I could get away with [guys] getting with me because "Oh, I didn't know, dude (how smart you were). I wasn't in your class, so … ." So yeah, we're looked at the same way, but I'm treated differently. I've got more experience that way because of the sports. The thing is, there are girls that are smart, but, like, have nothing else going for them … appearance-wise, and they have no interests. They have few friends.… I think the friends they do have are very close."

The Super Girl has emerged out of convergent social forces exerting pressures on girls and girlhood in the 21st century. She is an extension of the Good Girl and the Smart Girl but has been shaped by certain cultural forces—neoliberalism, and postfeminism in particular. Numerous feminist scholars have argued that girls and young women have been positioned as ideal neoliberal subjects (Bay-Cheng, 2015; Gill 2007; Gill 2008; Ringrose, 2007; Rutherford, 2018, among others). They are called on to "lean in" to opportunities for success, to focus on their individual growth and development, and to become productive members of a capitalist society. Such ideologies often overlap with postfeminism—claims that gender equality has been achieved, feminism is unnecessary, and girls are free to live agentic, autonomous lives (Rutherford, 2018). A "postfeminist sensibility" is evident in the media and includes the commodification of femininity, a focus on individualism, empowerment, sexualization, and consumerism (Gill, 2007).

Many have held up the Super Girl as evidence that feminism has achieved its aim of equality for girls/women. She is represented in media stories of girls ruling the world—stories that are reduced to one standard (unrealistic) format that presents high-achieving girls as happy and stress-free (Pomerantz and Raby, 2017). The Super Girl has been called by other names. Kindlon (2006) describes her as the "alpha girl"—the girl who is talented, motivated, and a confident leader. His book is steeped with postfeminist arguments, namely that the women's movement has done its job and equality has been achieved. He provides data regarding girls' and women's increased participation in education and career opportunities as evidence that today's girls can reap the benefits of the past women's movement. He asserts:

> "The alpha girl doesn't feel limited by her sex. She is a *person* first, and then a woman. Issues of sex and gender, dependence and independence, and domination and subordination are largely irrelevant to how she sees herself in the world."
>
> (p. xv)

Following Kindlon's logic, girls (and perhaps by extension, women) are only limited by experiences of sexism and misogyny if they *feel* limited by them. Ergo, it is all in our heads (or hearts). Further, girls can rise above these limitations if they simply choose to do so. By asserting that these alpha girls achieve success by seeing themselves as a *person* first, the implicit (and not so subtle) implication is that girls/women are not people. That we are something other than (less than?) a person.

The alpha girl (or Super Girl) is also positioned as the neoliberal subject—her focus is on how she sees herself, how she can succeed as an individual. The neoliberal ideology is based on the myth that the United States functions as a meritocracy, where people gain power and resources based on their merit and advancement is based on talent and hard work. The neoliberal belief is that this system is post-sexist (and post-racist, classist, etc.); therefore, girls and women have unfettered opportunities, and any challenges they face are self-imposed (Bay-Cheng, 2015). Thus, the Super Girl's strength resides in her motivation to lead, not to change structural issues that create domination and subordination.

Neoliberal feminism is a recent discourse about feminism, one that prioritizes work–life balance and the pursuit of "having it all" as the pathway toward, and evidence of, female empowerment (McRobbie, 2020; Rottenberg, 2018). The neoliberal feminist subject accepts full responsibility for her own well-being and self-care, which relies on her ability to juggle multiple obligations (for women, often framed as work-family balance) (2018). Thus, the feminist cannot "have it all" but must, in fact, "do it all"—in just the right proportions. Neoliberal feminism frames "all" women as equally oppressed and having equal access to the neoliberal dream (McRobbie, 2020). Neoliberal feminism carefully polices girls'/women's gendered presentation but also creates and enforces boundaries of race and social class (2020). Not everyone can possibly have it all.

Despite over a century of feminist movements within the United States and worldwide, gender stereotypes and gendered power dynamics persist. The legitimate feminist goals of empowering girls and young women have been co-opted by market forces, twisting these goals into new directions (Chaudhry, 2007). Although it might first appear that the Super Girl is a threat to patriarchy and existing power structures, we argue that she is allowed (and perhaps encouraged) to flourish because the expectations for perfection channel girls' energy—that might otherwise be used for direct resistance—into avenues that maintain the status quo. We argue that the Super Girl is allowed to excel in many areas because of the balance she retains regarding many traditional expectations of femininity. It is acceptable for her to be intelligent and outstanding but only if she toes the line in other ways. The Super Girl strives to counterbalance her academic and leadership strengths with traits and roles deemed more traditionally feminine. These notably include being physically attractive, friendly, and likable. Thus, the Super Girl can be smart, but not bookish; the boss, but not "bossy."

In many of our interviews, girls talked about ways they embrace the expectations of Super Girl and the belief that anything is possible for them. Even if they are aware of gender inequalities, they want to live up to the expectation that they will excel, that they will break the glass ceilings. Mr. Walker commented on how he saw girls navigate gender inequality:

> They just think, "If I work hard enough, forget those barriers—I'm gonna smash those." I can think of a number of students that I have in classes that really give off that vibe and attitude of, "I'm gonna go cure cancer, be a doctor. I'm gonna be a lawyer, maybe the governor, the flipping president." A lot of students give off that vibe.

How exactly do girls come to be Super Girls? In the next chapter, we explore the complicated interplay of agency and socialization in girls' lives in more nuance. As we have argued, we believe many cultural pressures encourage girls to adopt the Super Girl way of being. We spoke with girls and educators who also named some of the factors influencing girls' engagement with this set of unrealistic expectations. Educators and girls both articulated that educators expect girls to be super—to excel in school and extracurricular activities. Some educators endorse this model of the self-made Super Girl, as Mrs. Carter articulates here:

> Being really smart is great here. And … those students that tend to be in leadership and volunteering and stepping forward all the time are the ones that tend to be well-liked and well-known. And so then they become … [get] in[to] leadership positions, which then would classify them in that popular category. Because they worked hard, they're out there and they're putting themselves out there. Some of the kids that might be less popular are, probably, more shy.

Many cultural pressures and expectations that are explicitly gendered construct the Super Girl. Mrs. Taylor added, "The girl has to be everything and not only smart but thin and an athlete, which is really … interesting—that for the males, we tend to allow them to just be one or the other." It is not simply that the world is asking too much of *youth*; we ask too much of *girls*. Even while students and educators could speak to how the Super Girl expectation manifested inside the school, many noted that this was a phenomenon much more extensive than any single school environment. Mr. Walker describes how these pressures exist within a wider cultural context:

> So, I think for the gender roles and what they're expected at school, I think it's just, society as a whole sends a message. I see it less as Our Lady of Guadalupe as a school screaming that, than just more of culture … saying that.

What's the Catch?

Not all girls have the same access to become a Super Girl—some have more access to *choose* this route as an avenue to a fulfilling life. Even for those who can, there are numerous potential adverse consequences to their health and well-being. Pressures to conform to these constructs create and reinforce sexist, classist, racist, and homophobic attitudes and hold girls to unreasonable expectations. This often leads to more considerable distress and consequences to girls' well-being. In Chapter 3, we explore how girls navigate the costs and benefits associated with these expectations.

References

Bay-Cheng, L. Y. (2015). The agency line: A neoliberal metric for appraising young women's sexuality. *Sex Roles*, 73(7–8), 279–291.

Bian, L., Leslie, S. J., and Cimpian, A. (2017). Gender stereotypes about intellectual ability emerge early and influence children's interests. *Science*, 355(6323), 389–391. doi:10.1126/science.aah6524.

Bian, L., Leslie, S.J., and Cimpian, A. (2018). Evidence of bias against girls and women in contexts that emphasize intellectual ability. *American Psychologist, 73 (9)*, 1139–1153. doi:10.1037/amp0000427.supp (Supplemental).

Brown, L. M. (2003). *Girlfighting: Betrayal and rejection among girls*. New York University Press.

Chaudhry, L. (2007, May 1). The supergirl syndrome. *The Nation*. www.thenation.com/article/archive/supergirl-syndrome.

Chesney-Lind, M., and Irwin, K. (2008). *Beyond bad girls: Gender, violence and hype*. Routledge.

Gill, R. (2008). Culture and subjectivity in neoliberal and postfeminist times. *Subjectivity*, 25, 432–445.

Gill, R. (2007). Postfeminist media culture: Elements of a sensibility. *European Journal of Cultural Studies*, 10, 147–166. doi:10.1057/sub.2008.28.

Gonick, M. (2003). *Between femininities: Ambivalence, identity, and the education of girls*. SUNY Press.

Gonick, M., Renold, E., Ringrose, J., and Weems, L. (2009). Rethinking agency and resistance: What comes after girl power? *Girlhood Studies*, 2(2), 1–9. doi:10.3167/ghs.2009.020202.

Hinshaw, S., and Kranz, R. (2009). *The triple bind: Saving our teenage girls from today's pressures*. Ballantine Books.

Kindlon, D. and Thompson, M. (1999). *Raising Cain: Protecting the Emotional Life of Boys*. Ballantine Books.

Lamb, S. (2002). *The secret lives of girls: What good girls really do—sex play, aggression, and their guilt*. Simon & Schuster.

Lipkin, E. (2009). *Girls' Studies: Seal Studies*. Seal Press.

Manne, K. (2017). *Down girl: The logic of misogyny*. Oxford University Press.

McRobbie, A. (2020). *Feminism and the politics of resilience: Essays on gender, media and the end of welfare*. John Wiley & Sons.

Morris, M. (2016). *Pushout: The criminalization of Black girls in schools*. The New Press.

Muradoglu, M., Horne, Z., Hammond, M. D., Leslie, S.J., and Cimpian, A. (2021). Women—Particularly Underrepresented Minority Women—and Early-Career Academics Feel Like Impostors in Fields That Value Brilliance . *Journal of Educational Psychology*. (Advance online publication.) doi:10.1037/edu0000669.

Pomerantz, S. and Raby, R. (2017). *Smart girls: Success, school, and the myth of post-feminism*. University of California Press.

Raby, R. (2012). *School rules: Obedience, discipline, and elusive democracy*. University of Toronto Press.

Ringrose, J. (2007). Successful girls? Complicating post-feminist, neo-liberal discourses of educational achievement and gender equality. *Gender and Education*, 19(4), 471–489. doi:10.1080/09540250701442666.

Rottenberg, C. (2018). *The rise of neoliberal feminism*. Oxford University Press. doi:10.1093/oso/9780190901226.001.0001.

Rutherford, A. (2018). Feminism, psychology, and the gendering of neoliberal subjectivity: From critique to disruption. *Theory & Psychology*, 28(5), 619–644. doi:10.1177/0959354318797194.

Simmons, R. (2002). *Odd girl out: The hidden culture of aggression in girls*. Harcourt.

Simmons, R. (2009). *The curse of the good girl: Raising authentic girls with courage and confidence*. Penguin.

Storage, D., Charlesworth, T.E., Banaji, M.R., and Cimpian, A. (2020). Adults and children implicitly associate brilliance with men more than women. *Journal of Experimental Social Psychology*, 90, 104020. doi:10.1016/j.jesp.2020.104020.

Chapter 3

Gotta Get By

Conformity, Agency, and Survival

I mean, that's the way I view it. I'm very intelligent. I'm athletic. I'm the student body president. Like ... if you do it right you can work the system. I am the happiest I've ever been.

Grace, 12th grade

But so, I feel like they [girls] are all just stressed out [of] their marbles. But I think definitely gender expectations fit into this. So, I think—I don't think I can really speak to how society's pressures on them make them feel 'cause I feel like we haven't really addressed it in my class enough. But I feel like they're stressed and I think they feel pressure—just out the wazoo—of what's expected of them. And I just see the general worry and the general stress of cramming.

Mr. Walker

Conforming to others' expectations, school rules, and dominant discourses of femininity can be strategic forms of resilience (at least in the short term), allowing girls to survive within oppressive systems. We examine various survival strategies that emerged from our interviews, situating our investigation within a body of literature that challenges individualistic and neoliberal frames (Jokinen, 2016; Klocker, 2007). We scrutinize girls' so-called "choices" in the context of asking, "What is this girl really able to do and to be?" Further, we present a construct of "survival dissonance," describing how girls engage in narratives and cognitive framing of oppressive experiences that appear to minimize, excuse, or justify unjust circumstances. We argue that girls might engage in these ways of conceptualizing events in order to protect themselves. When embedded in oppressive systems that they do not feel they can change, the best defense of their sense of self and feelings of safety might be to reframe the situation as less harmful. We identify survival strategies among educators as well, whose accounts at times appeared dismissive of girls' experiences of oppression. We describe how their stories are embedded in larger narratives of powerlessness and learned helplessness.

DOI: 10.4324/9781003111535-4

Agency within Oppressive Systems

Throughout our work with girls (and educators), we sought to understand their experiences by honoring their agency while recognizing the limitations of that agency, given the restrictive contexts of their lives. As feminist researchers, we believe that any analysis of agency must account not only for gender, but race, class, sexual orientation, and other social identities that can restrict or expand agency. Exploring agency is complicated by the numerous ways the construct itself can be and has been interpreted within the research. Feminist scholars have explored possible differences in feelings about agency, being agentic, and being expected to be agentic (Rutherford, 2018). Feminist scholarship about the sexualization of girls has offered a nuanced exploration of girls' agency (see Edell et al., 2013; Renold and Ringrose, 2011; Ringrose, 2012). We agree with Renold and Ringrose, (2011), who call for researchers to see the complexity and difficulty for girls in navigating and performing "schizoid sexual subjectivities" and apply this call to theorizing about girls' experiences of oppression in school.

The emphasis on girls' agency is central to neoliberal and postfeminist narratives that have shaped the social pressures exerted on girls. A neoliberal frame encourages girls to take up a "mandate of uncritical individual choice" (Edell et al., 2013, p. 14). From a postfeminist frame, the belief in girls' agency and unconstricted choice are essential—they are posed as the preferable opposite of "victimhood" for girls (Rutherford, 2018). The idea that girls have a wide range of choices about who and how to be upholds the belief that girls are excelling, and feminist interventions are no longer necessary. Neoliberal and postfeminist sensibilities insist that the individual is a rational, self-reflexive agent who constructs their life narrative through choices they make (Gonick et al., 2009). We believe it is essential to trouble such straightforward claims of choice and to recognize that girls choose from an impoverished set of options confined by heteronormative, white, middle-class femininity (2009). Klocker (2007) distinguishes between "thick" and "thin" agency. Thick agency is when girls can take action in situations where they have a broad range of choices and options. By contrast, girls enact *thin* agency when making choices about their lives within very restrictive contexts where their opportunities are limited. We argue that girls employ thin agency when they choose to adopt the Good Girl, Smart Girl, or Super Girl narratives, as they are exercising such agency within a narrow frame of options available to them.

There is not one clear and direct path for exploring the ways girls (and educators) navigate agency. While we want to problematize and nuance conversations about choice, we do not want to fully abandon the "conceptual, material or political usefulness" of choice (Rutherford, 2018, p. 627). We seek to make sense of girls' experiences of critical agency (McRobbie, 2008) by analyzing their actions and discourses about their lives within the context of the circumstances and power dynamics within which they are embedded.

Choice is only helpful as a construct of analysis when considering the available options and the socio-political context. Further, teasing apart girls' decisions as "freely chosen" and indicative of agency from culturally imposed ideas could be an impossible task. Each of us actively constructs a sense of self. Thus, cultural norms and ideals become internalized, and we can experience them as self-generated rather than culturally imposed (Rutherford, 2018). "Gendered subjectivity is less about balances of agency (girl power) and compliance (girl victims) than it is about contingent and ambiguous practices of identity" (Gonick et al., 2009, p. 6). We do not position ourselves (as adults and researchers) as having an inherent or acquired ability to distinguish authentic "choice" or "agency" in these contexts. Instead, we work to hold the tensions, negotiations, uncertainties, and contradictions that result from mediated choices.

Conformity and Agency

In the following two sections of the book, we explore how girls (and educators) engage in the work of resistance and transformation within schools. In this chapter, we explore the myriad ways girls face social pressures, interpersonal sexism (and other -isms), and structural inequalities and how they respond in a manner that could be labeled "conformity." We nuance what "conforming" might include and explore the possibility that girls' conformity is an expression of agency within constricted contexts that demonstrates resilience.

As we describe in Chapter 2, Good Girls (and by extension, Super Girls) are expected to suppress their feelings and desires. Girls might appear to conform to these pressures while finding outlets for their feelings that go unnoticed by adults. For example, Good Girls are sexually modest and avoid expressions of overt sexuality. Being denied the ability to express one's sexuality outwardly does not mean that girls do not have sexual feelings—they might suppress them or engage in sexual activities in secret (Lamb, 2002).

Another way that girls enact agency while conforming to societal expectations of femininity is by managing conflicts. Good Girls are nice, caretakers of others' feelings, and do not engage in aggression. The social prohibition against conflicts with other girls does not prevent disputes, but it often leads girls to address their disagreements and problems in ways that are less visible to adults. A body of literature has emerged exploring these conflict methods, often termed "relational aggression" or "indirect aggression" (Brown, 2003; Simmons, 2002; Tanenbaum, 2011; Wiseman, 2003). In Phase 1 of our study with middle school girls, the students talked about avoiding direct conflicts with other girls because they did not want to hurt their feelings or get in trouble for having a conflict. They would find less direct ways to manage these conflicts or end friendships that had run their course.

Unfortunately, some scholars have presented girls' engagement in these forms of conflict as pathological and problematic. Such narratives work to further construct the Good Girl by juxtaposing the Bad Girl (or mean girl). Labeling some girls (and some behaviors) as "bad" can further clarify the expectations for how Good Girls should behave. The focus on Bad Girls as having "gone awry" emphasizes individual girls and not the systems they exist within. "The discovery of girls' aggression has just handed girls more bad news about themselves and more reasons to blame the problems of misogyny on other girls rather than pervasive institutional sexism" (Chesney-Lind and Irwin, 2008, p. 124). In contrast, as Brown (2003) describes, "girlfighting" can be understood as a response to a world that teaches girls there is a limited amount of access to power—that girls have less access than boys. Thus, girls learn to fight over a small slice of the "patriarchal pie" in a way that is allowed. Engaging in alternative methods of conflict (different from the way that boys fight or the way that "bad" girls fight) is an enactment of agency within a restricted system.

Costs of Conformity

The Super Girl is the empowered neoliberal subject. She works hard for her accomplishments and overcomes barriers and obstacles. The structural forces that limit her options based on sexism, racism, heterosexism, and classism are impeded by the emphasis on individual agency. As Bay-Cheng (2015) writes about girls' sexual agency, "What appears to be an expanded, liberated space is actually a minefield, one that requires continual self-monitoring, impression management, and a full complement of defensive and offensive maneuvers" (p. 286). We assert that this minefield extends to many other areas of girls' lives, including the pressures to be Super.

Girls currently face a "Triple Bind" culture (Hinshaw and Kranz, 2009). They are expected to be good at all the traditional feminine traits, be good at most things considered traditionally masculine, and conform to narrow, unrealistic standards regarding beauty and sexuality. It might look to some that girls have a wealth of choices, but ultimately, the expectations placed on them might be impossible to meet. Girls and women find they can either be well-liked or respected, but rarely both (2009).

Martin (2007) describes what she calls the "duty to excel"—that girls should strive to achieve "effortless perfection." Many models of resilience neglect to acknowledge the violence experienced by girls who do succeed. The standards for perfection demand ongoing sacrifices of the self. Herein lies what McRobbie (2020) calls the "tyranny of the perfect." The expectations to excel at everything creates overscheduled and overtaxed lives that set girls up for emotional distress. "The 'perfect' carries with it violent intent, not just in its racial and class-based exclusionary effect, but also in its acts of inclusion for those directly within its embrace" (McRobbie, 2020, p. 52). Girls who have access to become a Super Girl face certain pressures and expectations. Girls for whom such perfect status—owing to their race, social class, etc.—is unattainable might find relative freedom in outsider status.

One of the most insidious aspects of the Super Girl life is the demand for perfection—and perfection that looks effortless. Girls know that this image is cultivated. Olivia (12th grade) describes this tension between the real and the produced:

> I feel like women are supposed to live a perfect life. And then you see on Instagram and stuff that where it's like...everything looks natural [and] candid, but you know it's posed. It just seems like everyone is turned on—like, you have to have that switch, and it's mainly for women, I think.

Simmons (2009) argues that the expectations to be a Good Girl can erode one's ability to cope with stress. Attempts to conform to the Good Girl standard can cut girls off from the full range of human emotions—anger in particular—and make it difficult for girls to set boundaries or challenge unjust rules. Being always expected to be kind and selfless can limit girls' expressions of their own needs. Empathy for others combined with self-denial can lead to anxiety and depression (Hinshaw and Kranz, 2009). Without permission to express themselves honestly, girls might turn their feelings inward and experience depression or engage in self-harming behaviors.

Unfortunately, Good Girls might be invisible within school systems and taken for granted as compliant or not causing problems. Narratives about Super Girls succeeding without any difficulties impact how educators conceptualize, interact with, and allocate resources to girls. As a result, their mental health needs are neglected by adults both inside and outside schools. Good Girls might feel so much pressure to be perfect that they struggle in private and avoid asking for help. "A girl who never seems to do anything wrong might be choosing to make her mistakes in private, becoming secretive, ashamed, or self-destructive" (Simmons, 2009; p. 11). In their interviews with girls who self-identified as academically successful, Pomerantz and Raby (2017) found that the girls shared stories about how they manage and negotiate the emotional and social costs of high achievement and shared their concerns about their futures. A few of the educators we spoke with expressed concerns about how the pressures to be Super Girls impact their students. As we saw with one of the quotes opening this chapter, Mr. Walker discussed his worries about the amount of stress he heard from his female students. Another teacher, Mr. Hill, describes the pressures that girls face:

> When I think about it, [it] seems that those students that are more concerned and maybe more affected by the stress of trying to do all of

> these things seem to be more girls than boys. And ... I'm wondering if that is because they feel more pressured to do that than the boys do.

Ms. Powell also talked about her worries about girls taking on too much and the impact it has on them:

> I have just exactly that concern with some of them [the girls in her classes]. I'm like, don't you think you're taking on a little too much here? You know ... you don't have to be perfect at everything. The world's not gonna quit spinning if you let go of the reins for a while and, you know, that kind of thing. I've mentioned it because it does concern me that they feel like they have to do everything. It's just unrealistic and ... at some point, they're going to burn out.

We believe that these educators have good reason to be concerned about the stress that girls face and the consequences to their overall well-being, including their mental health. A recent report from the Centers for Disease Control and Prevention (CDC) (2019) found one in three high school students reported persistent feelings of sadness or hopelessness—a 40% increase from 2009. The groups that endorsed these feelings most often were lesbian, gay, bisexual, and female-identifying students. The report also indicated that suicidality (ranging from ideation to attempts) has increased since 2009. Specifically, one in six students shared that they had made a suicide plan in the past year—this represents a 44 percent increase from 2009. About half of lesbian, gay and bisexual (LGB) students indicated serious suicidal consideration and Black students' suicide attempts increased by almost 50 percent between 2009 and 2019. The CDC also reports that 9.4% of two- to 17-year-olds have ADHD diagnoses, 7.4% have a behavioral diagnosis, 7.1% have been diagnosed with an anxiety disorder, and 3.2% have been diagnosed with depression.

Research has demonstrated that the gender discrepancy in depressive disorder diagnoses begins in adolescence (Breslau et al., 2017). Recently researchers have investigated risk factors for the first onset of depressive disorder in a community sample of adolescent girls (Michelini et al., 2021). Participants included 479 girls aged 13.5–15.5 years with no history of depressive disorders and who were assessed over 3 years. Factors found to contribute to the first onset of depression were: depressive symptoms, rumination, parental mood disorder, and parental criticism. Salk et al. (2016) conducted a longitudinal study examining differences in age and prevalence of depression diagnoses and looked at chronicity (days spent in a depressive episode). They found disparities in rates of adolescent depression according to gender (which emerged at 13–14 years) and found similarities in days spent in depressive episodes. Tolman et al. (2006) found "powerful evidence that early adolescent girls who internalize conventional femininity ideologies, particularly regarding body objectification, have lower self-esteem and higher depressed mood" (p. 91). The role that stereotypical femininity or pressures to be a Super Girl play in developing mental health issues is worth further consideration, particularly in light of rising rates of mental health struggles.

It's also worth considering how identity development manifests in girls' internalized messaging about conformity, success, and perfection. Adolescence is famously (or infamously) referred to as the stage of identity development and formation when questions of "who am I" and "who am I to become" are at the forefront (Erikson, 1968). While Erikson's theory of identity formation calls for situating that development in context, the costs or consequences of the pressure girls feel to conform to stereotypes of femininity (or to negotiate the Smart Girl, Good Girl, Super Girl prototypes) is neglected in the research. Significant evidence exists demonstrating the negative impact of sexualization on girls' mental health (Lamb and Koven, 2019). The connection between women's experiences of harassment and mental health distress has also been documented in the literature (Hackett et al., 2019, among others).

In our studies, we continue to reflect on the experiences of the participants and ask: How is identity development (exploration and commitment to different aspects of identity development) impacted by pressure to conform to gender stereotypes or Super Girl aspirations? There is clear evidence based in minority stress theory (Meyer, 2003) that links mental health disparities of LGB youth to the chronic stress that accompanies systematic bias, harassment, and discrimination (Burton et al., 2013; Fulginiti et al., 2020). These studies point to the importance of considering intersecting identities in the contexts of discrimination and harassment during adolescent development (Goldbach and Gibbs, 2017).

Surviving Within Oppressive Systems

Survival Dissonance

One of the patterns that emerged in our interviews with girls is a concept we have termed "survival dissonance." We conceptualize survival dissonance as a specific manifestation of cognitive dissonance (Festinger, 1957). According to cognitive dissonance theory, individuals often feel discomfort when they experience inconsistencies in their thinking, values, or behaviors or when they participate in an action that goes against one or more of their values. People are often motivated to eliminate this discomfort and use a range of strategies to do so. According to this theory, people often want to restore what is called cognitive consonance—such that their actions, beliefs, and thoughts are well aligned. Depending on the situation and the options available to them, a person might attempt to resolve the conflict by changing their behavior, ignoring or disbelieving a new source of contradictory information, or changing their ideas or beliefs about something. If they cannot change the situation they are facing or behave differently, people will often unconsciously adjust the way they think about it. We draw upon cognitive dissonance and apply it within settings where an individual might be trying to "survive" harmful or oppressive conditions.

We see survival dissonance occurring when girls experience sexism, misogyny, and other forms of oppressive systems, structures, and individuals in schools. When girls feel that they do not have the power to change the school system or alter the behavior of a powerful agent who is creating the oppression, one way to resolve this is to reframe their understanding of the situation. In the next section of the book, we explore girls' and educators' engagement in resistance in response to oppression. However, we know that resistance is not always possible. Individuals might decide not to directly confront an incident of bias if they determine that the potential costs will outweigh the benefits (Brinkman et al., 2011; Brinkman and Manning, 2016). We argue that girls and educators engage in a cost-benefit analysis to decide when, if, and how to respond to sexism and other forms of oppression. In situations where one does not speak up about oppression, one might experience cognitive dissonance. In one study where participants were exposed to sexism, some of the women who did not confront the perpetrator sought to reduce the cognitive dissonance caused by altering their beliefs about the nature of the bias (Rasinski et al., 2013). In particular, they reframed the perpetrator in a relatively positive light and interpreted his actions as being less harmful.

When embedded in oppressive systems that girls do not feel they can change, it might be most protective of their sense of self and their understanding of their own safety to reframe the situation as less harmful. Thus, survival dissonance emerges. In these instances, we found that girls and educators engaged in various cognitive strategies to decrease their dissonance—including justifying sexist school policies, minimizing the harm of experiences of oppression, and interpreting the actors' intentions with beneficence. For example, Rebecca (11th grade) discussed her experiences with a male administrator in the school. She held a role in student life that included assisting him with preparation for school activities. She described how he treated her differently from the boys in school:

> So, I think there's times where he feels like he can't trust me with something because I'm a girl or I can't lift this or…I get that is [a] safety precaution, but I think sometimes he just doubts me a little bit.

She shared this as an example of unfair treatment, and even as she described it, she tries to justify his behavior as rooted in "safety." She goes on to describe that he treats female educators similarly, saying that his treatment isn't "just with her":

INTERVIEWER: Why do you think or what's your sense of, like, why he's maybe like that with you and with this other woman?

REBECCA: Just 'cause he's kind of in charge on campus. His job entails everything that students do outside of academia. And I know he's a very busy man, but I think he definitely likes to show his authority sometimes or he doesn't show it the right way. I wouldn't say there's a thing mainly towards women—it's not actually, it's not constant. [It] could be way worse. I would say our administration is very full of male dominance.

Rebecca describes her attempts to have a good relationship with this administrator and the need to do so given her job in the school. She describes her role in the school as being very meaningful to her, so it would be a loss for her to give up that role to distance herself from this man. What else is she to do, other than an attempt to make sense of his behavior as "not that bad"? There is an incredible power imbalance between them, so it seems unrealistic to expect her to confront him directly. Since the administrator treats his female peers the same way, why would Rebecca expect that as a student, she could get him to treat her any better?

Learned Helplessness

Another possible dynamic emerges when one is faced with a situation they do not agree with, but feel powerless to control—learned helplessness. Both students and educators can experience learned helplessness, but we focus specifically on educators' experiences with this phenomenon. Some situations occur within the schools where it appears that educators are condoning sexism, misogyny, and other forms of oppression. At times, they are indeed condoning, reinforcing, and even promoting such experiences. As we explicate throughout the book, the male administrators at Our Lady of Guadalupe developed numerous policies and practices which led to discriminatory experiences for the girls (and often the adult women) in the school.

However, we recognize the possibility that some actions (or inactions) on the part of educators do not signal their acceptance of oppression but instead result from learned helplessness. The theory of learned helplessness (Seligman, 1972) suggests that individuals who face uncontrollable challenging or traumatic experiences might experience emotional distress and engage in a passive response to the events. Educators who work in systems where they are repeatedly told that the school cannot or will not prevent or adequately respond to sexism, sexual violence, racism, sexual harassment, and toxic masculinity might "learn" that they are helpless to do anything about these incidents. Educators who speak up and engage in advocacy with and on behalf of their students could face backlash from unsupportive administrators. When this happens, educators might become less active in the face of oppression, not wanting to make a situation worse for themselves or their students.

Educators might also face personal discrimination within the same school system and feel helpless to support their students when they cannot change the conditions they themselves are facing. Ms. Lewis shared, "I have had interactions with parents where that's been an issue—not so much sexually harassed, but I guess somewhat. And ... the administration did not have my back, but that's, I think because it's a parent." When asked whether girls are treated unfairly in the school, Ms. Jackson describes her own experiences of sexism within the school:

> So, I can't really speak about any students who have been in, I don't know, a weird situation because of being a girl. But ... something that I've noticed as a female teacher is how some of the other teachers who do happen to be male ... address me, just saying, "Hey Kiddo," instead of saying, "Hello, Ms. Jackson." Or [they just say], "Hey." I'm just being called a name that's less professional and friendly.

When a female teacher is treated disrespectfully by the administration, it is difficult to imagine that she would feel confident standing up for the girls in the school. This teacher shared many of her concerns about the mistreatment of girls in the school but often felt unable to take action to change the conditions that the girls faced. Ms. Jackson shared how she is left out of important conversations happening within the school:

> This is, again, this is just my perception, but I feel like the administration don't [*sic*] say things to me or choose to say things differently to me because I'm a girl. I think they see me as, "Oh, she's nice." But they don't have serious conversations with me, whereas they'll talk to my male colleagues about issues typically instead of going to me.

When teachers experience sexual harassment, sexism, racism, and homophobia, it becomes difficult for them to transform the environments to improve them for students.

Learned helplessness might appear to the outsider as acceptance of sexist policies or practices but reflects a more profound, complicated experience on the part of the educator. Educators who are deeply committed to their jobs might remain in problematic school systems because of their dedication to the role. They might decide to tolerate some dynamics to stay in their positions. In the third section of this book, we explore in more depth the experiences of educators and the importance of their own healing in order to be supportive advocates for girls.

Unintended Consequences

Experiencing survival dissonance or learned helplessness in response to sexism and other forms of discrimination within school systems are understandable reactions. When a girl is faced with sexist treatment in school and cannot change or leave the situation, it makes sense that she would try to accept the conditions. Thinking to oneself, "Well, maybe it wasn't *that* bad what he said or did" can help a student cope with the situation, at least temporarily. But what happens when it turns out that it *was* that bad? If the perpetrator continues to engage in the same types of sexist behaviors? When someone realizes that they were poorly treated by another, and then minimized or explained away the behavior, they might feel even worse. What if the perpetrator then engages in the same behavior toward other girls? Girls might experience guilt when they realize that they justified behavior that caused harm to themselves and others.

Further, survival dissonance in response to sexism in schools might have the unfortunate consequence of *increasing* sexist beliefs or behaviors in the school setting. Unfortunately, when someone does not confront sexism or other forms of oppression, it could send the message that the belief or behavior is acceptable. Raskinski et al. (2013) argue that some target group members who respond passively to sexism might come to see the perpetrator more favorably (via dissonance reduction). As a result, they might engage in more positive behaviors toward the perpetrator, which might reinforce such biased behavior in the perpetrator and potential bystanders. The good news is that research suggests that confronting perpetrators of sexism can decrease bias in the future (Mallet and Wagner, 2011). In the next section of this book, we explore girls' and educators' resistance to sexism and other forms of oppression within schools.

References

Bay-Cheng, L.Y. (2015). The agency line: A neoliberal metric for appraising young women's sexuality. *Sex Roles*, 73(7–8),279–291.

Breslau, J., Gilman, S.E., Stein, B.D., Ruder, T., Gmelin, T., and Miller, E. (2017). Sex differences in recent first-onset depression in an epidemiological sample of adolescents. *Translational Psychiatry*, 7(5), e1139. doi:10.1038/tp.2017.105.

Brinkman, B.G., Garcia, K., and Rickard, K.M. (2011). "What I wanted to do was…": Discrepancies between college women's desired and reported responses to gender prejudice. *Sex Roles*, 65, 344–355. doi:10.1007/s11199-011-0020-7.

Brinkman, B.G. and Manning, L. (2016). Children's intended responses to gender-based bullying as targets and bystanders. *Childhood*, 23(2), 221–235. doi:10.1177/0907568215595095.

Brown, L.M. (2003). *Girlfighting: Betrayal and rejection among girls*. New York University Press.

Burton, C., Marshal, M., Chisolm, D., Sucato, G., and Friedman, M. (2013). Sexual Minority-Related Victimization as a Mediator of Mental Health Disparities in Sexual Minority Youth: A Longitudinal Analysis. *Journal of Youth & Adolescence*, 42(3), 394–402. doi:10.1007/s10964-012-9901-5.

Centers for Disease Control and Prevention. (2019). *Youth risk behavior survey: Data summary and trends report 2009–2019*. www.cdc.gov/healthyyouth/data/yrbs/pdf/YRBSDataSummaryTrendsReport2019-508.pdf.

Chesney-Lind, M. and Irwin, K. (2008). *Beyond bad girls: Gender, violence and hype*. Routledge.

Edell, D., Brown, L.M., and Tolman, D. (2013). Embodying sexualisation: When theory meets practice in intergenerational feminist activism. *Feminist Theory*, 14(3), 275–284. doi:10.1177/1464700113499844.

Erikson, E.H. (1968). *Identity: Youth and crisis* (No. 7). W.W. Norton & Company.

Festinger, L. (1957). *A Theory of Cognitive Dissonance* (Vol. 2). Stanford University Press.

Festinger, L. (1962). Cognitive dissonance. *Scientific American*. 207(4): 93–107. doi:10.1038/scientificamerican1062–1093.

Fulginiti, A. et al. (2021). Sexual minority stress, mental health symptoms, and suicidality among LGBTQ youth accessing crisis services. *Journal of Youth and Adolescence*, 50(5), 893–905. doi:10.1007/s10964-020-01354-3.

Goldbach, J. T. and Gibbs, J.J. (2017). A developmentally informed adaptation of minority stress for sexual minority adolescents. *Journal of Adolescence*, 55, 36–50. doi:10.1016/j.adolescence.2016.12.007.

Gonick, M., Renold, E., Ringrose, J., and Weems, L. (2009). Rethinking agency and resistance: What comes after girl power? *Girlhood Studies*, 2(2), 1–9. doi:10.3167/ghs.2009.020202.

Hackett, R.A., Steptoe, A., and Jackson, S.E. (2019). Sex discrimination and mental health in women: A prospective analysis. *Health Psychology*, 38(11), 1014–1024. doi:10.1037/hea0000796.supp (Supplemental).

Hinshaw, S. and Kranz, R. (2009). *The triple bind: Saving our teenage girls from today's pressures*. Ballantine Books.

Jokinen, E. (2016). Precarious everyday agency. *European Journal of Cultural Studies*, 19(1), 85–99.

Klocker, N. (2007). An example of 'thin'agency: Child domestic workers in Tanzania. In *Global perspectives on rural childhood and youth* (pp. 100–111). Routledge.

Lamb, S. (2002). *The secret lives of girls: What good girls really do—sex play, aggression, and their guilt*. Simon & Schuster.

Lamb, S. and Koven, J. (2019). Sexualization of girls: Addressing criticism of the APA report, presenting new evidence. *Sage Open*, 9(4), 1–15. doi:10.1177/215824401988102.

Mallett, R.K. and Wagner, D.E. (2011). The unexpectedly positive consequences of confronting sexism. *Journal of Experimental Social Psychology*, 47(1), 215–220. doi:10.1016/j.jesp.2010.10.001.

Martin, C.E. (2007). *Perfect girls, starving daughters: The frightening new normalcy of hating your body*. Simon & Schuster.

McRobbie, A. (2008). Young women and consumer culture: An intervention. *Cultural studies*, 22(5), 531–550.

McRobbie, A. (2020). *Feminism and the politics of resilience: Essays on gender, media and the end of welfare*. John Wiley & Sons.

Meyer, I. H. (2003). Prejudice as stress: Conceptual and measurement problems. *American Journal of Public Health*, 93(2), 262–265. doi:10.2105/AJPH.93.2.262.

Michelini, G. et al. (2021). Multiple domains of risk factors for first onset of depression in adolescent girls. *Journal of Affective Disorders*, 283, 20–29. doi:10.1016/j.jad.2021.01.036.

Pomerantz, S. and Raby, R. (2017). *Smart girls: Success, school, and the myth of post-feminism*. University of California Press.

Rasinski, H.M., Geers, A.L., and Czopp, A.M. (2013). "I guess what he said wasn't that bad": Dissonance in nonconfronting targets of prejudice. *Personality and Social Psychology Bulletin*, 39(7), 856–869. doi:10.1177/0146167213484769.

Renold, E. and Ringrose, J. (2011). Schizoid subjectivities? Re-theorizing teen girls' sexual cultures in an era of 'sexualization'. *Journal of sociology*, 47(4), 389–409.

Ringrose, Jessica. (2012). *Postfeminist education?: Girls and the sexual politics of schooling*. Routledge.

Rutherford, A. (2018). Feminism, psychology, and the gendering of neoliberal subjectivity: From critique to disruption. *Theory & Psychology*, 28(5), 619–644. doi:10.1177/0959354318797194.

Salk, R.H., Petersen, J.L., Abramson, L.Y., and Hyde, J.S. (2016). The contemporary face of gender differences and similarities in depression throughout adolescence: Development and chronicity. *Journal of Affective Disorders*, 205, 28–35. doi:10.1016/j.jad.2016.03.071.

Seligman, M.E. (1972). Learned helplessness. *Annual Review of Medicine*, 23(1), 407–412. doi:10.1146/annurev.me.23.020172.002203.

Simmons, R. (2002). *Odd girl out: The hidden culture of aggression in girls*. Harcourt.

Simmons, R. (2009). *The curse of the good girl: Raising authentic girls with courage and confidence*. Penguin.

Tanenbaum, L. (2011). *Catfight: Women and competition*. Seven Stories Press.

Tolman, D.L., Impett, E.A., Tracy, A.J., and Michael, A. (2006). Looking good, sounding good: Femininity ideology and adolescent girls' mental health. *Psychology of Women Quarterly*, 30(1), 85–95. doi:10.1111/j.1471-6402.2006.00265.x.

Wiseman, R. (2003). *Queen bees and wannabes: Helping your daughter survive cliques, boyfriends, gossip, and other realities of adolescence*. The Crown Publishing Group.

Chapter 4

Resistance to Gender Stereotypes and Sexism

I'm definitely a person that if someone says something that I don't agree with or I feel uncomfortable about, I'm like, "Just stop."

Tina, 12th grade

One method of creating conditions in schools where girls can thrive involves supporting their resistance strategies. Resistance to stereotypical expectations of femininity can thicken girls' agency (Klocker, 2007) by widening the range of options available to them about how to perform "girl." We conceptualize resistance on a continuum from vocalized critiques to direct, assertive action. We do not frame resistance as being *distinct from* resilience but rather often a *manifestation of* resilience. We conceptualize resistance as active, fluid, and negotiated. Girls explore methods of resistance while considering what options are available to them and weighing the potential costs and benefits of action.

Gender Role Stereotypes

Traditional stereotypes about gender place limitations and restrictions on ideas about what girls can do and who they can be. Gender role stereotypes are informed by the sociopolitical landscape and they intersect with stereotypes about race, class, and sexual orientation and change over time. Girls are given messages from parents, educators, peers, and the wider society (conveyed through many cultural artifacts, including the media) that they should "do gender" in particular ways to meet the expectations of gender role stereotypes (West and Zimmerman, 1987). Data from an international study suggest that gendered expectations shape girls' lives worldwide, exerting pressures even in early adolescence (Blum et al., 2017). Gendered expectations are conveyed through direct verbal messages about appropriate behavior for girls and indirectly through adults modeling gendered behavior. Children are often rewarded for engaging in what is deemed gender-appropriate behavior and punished if they step too far outside the norms (Coltrane, 1998; Lytton and Romney, 1991; Risman, 1998). Children can also develop traditional gender

DOI: 10.4324/9781003111535-5

role schemas through exposure to the media, including television (Shilo, 2021). Bem (1993) argued that through these socialization processes, cultural messages shape the way children view gender and they develop a cognitive schema for gender which influences their own gender identity.

A body of literature has explored several ways that traditional feminine ideologies and stereotypes place limits on girls (and women). Some common elements of these ideologies include the expectation that girls and women will be submissive, modest, nurturing, sensitive, invested in their appearance, and simultaneously sultry and chaste (Mahalik et al., 2005). According to Tolman (2009), two factors in feminine ideology—inauthenticity in relationships (notions of "playing nice," avoiding conflict, suppressing anger) and body objectification—have been implicated in adolescent girls' and young women's decision-making about their bodies. As a result, these factors have been associated with lower self-esteem and poor sexual health in girls and young women (Impett et al., 2006; Tolman, 2009). Endorsement of rigid feminine ideologies is related to decreased sexual-risk knowledge, decreased body esteem during sex, decreased sexual assertiveness, and lower levels of self-efficacy about using condoms (Curtin et al., 2011). Women who endorse feminine norms, especially the standards for beauty and romance, are more likely to adopt an objectified self-view (Siegel and Calogero, 2019). For girls, the internalization of a thin body as ideal is a significant predictor of body dissatisfaction, which itself is a risk factor in the onset of eating pathology and depression (Lawler and Nixon, 2010). Not surprisingly, body dissatisfaction is also associated with low self-esteem and abnormal eating habits (Mäkinen et al., 2012). Cultural pressures placed on girls to succumb to traditional gender roles generally increase in late childhood and often include being ladylike and dependent. These pressures can limit girls' sense of mastery and autonomy, which often results in a loss of self-esteem (Norman, 2000; Turner et al., 1995; Werner and Smith, 1982). However, as we discuss in this chapter, resistance to traditional feminine stereotypes can help protect girls against some of these adverse outcomes.

Numerous theories pose explanations about how children develop a gender identity (and how they carry this identity into adulthood). We will not review the theories here, but we refer the reader to our earlier work on gender identity development (Brinkman et al., 2014). We argue that children exert agency over their gender presentation and that a child's gender identity develops as part of a dynamic and complex negotiation process. Children act and react to gender role socialization, including experiences of sexism and gender prejudice. Children internalize gender role stereotypes (Schaffer, 2000), recognize the limitations of these stereotypes, challenge the stereotypes, and are aware of the consequences of not conforming to gendered expectations (Brinkman et al., 2010).

There are benefits to resisting the limitations of traditional gender stereotypes. People who endorse instrumental and active traits (commonly seen as masculine traits) have higher self-esteem and less anxiety and depression, and those with nurturing, expressive traits (sometimes considered feminine) demonstrate better communication skills and have greater relationship satisfaction (Bosow, 2006). Adults who endorse having both "masculine" and "feminine" traits have the most behavioral flexibility in both their work and interpersonal relationships (Bosow, 2006). These adults can take on leadership positions within their career setting and be nurturing and empathic in interpersonal relationships.

What Is Resistance?

Feminist scholars have explored various ways girls enact resistance to sexism and fight against the voices that endorse silence, passivity, ignorance, and weakness (Brown et al., 2007; Hinshaw and Kranz, 2009; Orenstein, 2011). Resistance is expressed in girls' anger and determination to resist the constraints of traditional femininity (Brown, 1998). One purpose of our intervention with girls at St. Bernadette's was to understand how they were resisting sexism and offer them tools to support that resistance. Our goal was not to establish an expectation that girls should or could always resist oppression. In fact, we acknowledge the very real barriers and risks of such resistance and the necessity to make cost-benefit analyses of resistance. Rather, our goal was to offer a thickening of girls' agency regarding sexism. We created an intervention that was meant to provide girls with information about sexism and strategies for navigating sexism to expand their ideas of the choices available to them. We sought to provide them with a wider range of options from which they would explore, choose, reject, negotiate, define, and redefine things in their own identity development projects.

During Phase 2 of our project we continued to explore girls' narratives about resistance to sexism and other forms of oppression within schools, as well as examining how educators made sense of girls' resistance strategies. What exactly is resistance? What does it look like? What does it feel like? How do others respond to girls' resistance in schools? We explored a continuum of resistance to sexism and other forms of oppression that girls experience within schools. Specifically, we hope to bring light to aspects of resistance that might be subtle but inform the ways girls seek to navigate the pressures surrounding gender.

Labeling Sexism

Research conducted with adult women has indicated that labeling an experience as gender prejudice or harassment is significantly correlated with responding assertively to such events (Bergman et al., 2002). Research with college students and adult populations indicates that women often do not label experiences as sexism or as harassment. For example, one study found that only 20–30% of a sample of 689 women self-labeled their experiences of sexual harassment (Magley, Hulin, Fitzgerald, and DeNardo, 1999). The process that individuals use to determine whether to label an experience is multi-faceted (Magley and Shupe, 2005) and there are numerous reasons girls and women might avoid naming sexism or sexual harassment. However, labeling an experience as harassment has been positively correlated with assertive responses (Bergman, Langhout, Palmieri, Cortina, and Fitzgerald, 2002), so it appears to be an important aspect of resistance to sexism. Education about sexism can increase girls' abilities to identify and label such events when they do take place, helping them cope with these events by externalizing the source of the problem. One goal of the intervention we developed at St. Bernadette's was to help girls recognize that they were not alone in experiencing many of the negative incidents they described and that these occurrences were a result of systemic sexism and oppression.

Learning to name sexism has taken place through consciousness-raising groups, within feminist classrooms, during feminist clubs and organizations, and is an element of programs designed to combat sexism. Within these environments, people learn about how sexism functions within society and can then connect their own experiences to this knowledge. For example, students taking women's or gender studies courses increase their awareness of prejudice (Malkin and Stake, 2004; Sevelius and Stake, 2003) and sexism in society (Howe, 1985; Stake, 2007). Programs for girls which focus on empowerment (like the one we developed) can also teach girls how to label sexism by learning to conceptualize their experiences within the context of their gendered position in societal systems that have failed them.

Programs for girls that emphasize collective empowerment and critical consciousness can increase girls' awareness of structural inequalities (Goodkind, Brinkman, and Elliott, 2020). The *critical consciousness* model describes how oppressed groups learn to critically analyze their social conditions and act to change them (Watts et al., 2011). There are three elements of critical consciousness: 1) critical reflection, which refers to a social analysis and moral rejection of societal inequities; 2) political efficacy, which is the perceived capacity to effect social and political change; and 3) critical action, which refers to individual or collective action taken to change institutional policies and practices. Increasing critical reflection among girls offers a way to engage in critical analysis that situates their experiences of sexism within the social context. Girls can then resist sexism because they are able to name it as something bigger than themselves. They might make more structural attributions to their experiences of sexism, rather than interpreting events as being personal.

Molly participated in the intervention at St. Bernadette's starting when she was in 6th grade and continued in the program until 11th grade. During her interview in 6th grade, when asked about experiences of being treated differently because she was a girl, she stated, "I don't think that's happened to me." In the interview in 11th grade, she stated that the program had increased her awareness and her ability to notice and label sexism:

> Well, I guess I'm more aware of things. I didn't notice things too much in 6th grade when we first started, and then … I actually started to notice things like the difference between what teachers prefer, like, boys or girls.

Critical Conformity

Additionally, girls' resistance can take the form of analyzing and critiquing gender expectations, while deciding to engage in the activity they were critiquing. This is a phenomenon we name as *critical conformity*. This might not always appear to be resistance, but we argue it has important distinctions from conformity without a critical analysis. As we discuss in Chapter 3, girls navigate agency within restricted contexts and weigh potential costs and benefits to their choices. Thus, girls might choose to engage in some behavior that is aligned with gender role expectations, while naming that there are negative aspects or consequences of that behavior. We saw numerous examples of girls in our study enacting critical conformity. For example, Olivia (12th grade) talked about the expectations that girls (and women) should look effortlessly perfect—one aspect of the Super Girl persona:

> One of the big things is the whole "no makeup makeup look." [laughter] It's like you have to look like you're not wearing makeup, but you're wearing like 25 different products. It's so stressful because if you don't have it perfect, then it will break through this facade that you just have this naturally beautiful—it's really stressful, but it's like, even if there's so much effort in taking a simple picture to put on Instagram … to make it seem candid is, like, the hardest part. [laughter]

Olivia recognized the commodification of the "no makeup makeup look"—the excessive number of products you are expected to purchase to pull this off—and the difficulty of exerting that much effort but attempting to appear effortless. While she critiqued this cultural practice and laughed as she described it, she did *not* say that she refuses to participate in it. In fact, her quote insinuates that she does practice such impression management herself—however stressful it might be. We read her quote to mean that she engages in this practice with open eyes—with the awareness that it is, in fact, a performance, and one that is *expected* of women.

Prove Them Wrong

Girls in both phases of our project demonstrated resistance to oppression by refusing to be confined by gender role stereotypes or limited in their behavior based on others' expectations. Several middle school girls described being told they could not play sports with the boys because they were girls. Sometimes they responded by saying they would find a way to play and prove them wrong—demonstrate to the boys that they were good enough to join. Kathleen (6th grade) shared her frustrations with the boys in her class refusing to pass the ball to her during games:

> No, usually, I kind of talk to them and tell them, like, "Hey, I want to be passed the ball" and stuff, and finally, when I do [get the ball], they realize that I'm pretty good. I want to go play football, and I want to do wrestling, and so, I can kind of show them that I'm not a weakling like they say I am.

It has been well established in the research literature that beliefs about gender-specific roles and responsibilities—gender role beliefs—are related to career and vocational aspirations as well as educational choices (Eccles, 1987; Schoon and Parsons, 2002). More recent research (Dicke, Safavian, and Eccles, 2019) has focused on the connection between gender role beliefs and science, technology, engineering, and mathematics (STEM) careers. Specifically, these researchers used longitudinal data to look at traditional work- and family-related gender role beliefs (TGRB) in adolescence concerning educational paths and STEM careers. Results showed that TGRB in adolescence could predict occupation for participants in their 40s. Traditional gender role beliefs predicted lower educational attainment and a lower chance of being in STEM fields. Many of the girls we interviewed in high school described their future career goals involving traditionally male-dominated fields, including entering military academies, and interest in branches of medicine (neuroscience/neurology) that still have gender disparities.

Many of the girls we interviewed articulated their awareness that being female could become a barrier for them on their career paths. Addison (12th grade) said:

> I think it's going to be hard physically and mentally going into the [Air Force] Academy, and I think, you know, being a girl is going to be very difficult because it's like a four-to-one ratio and you're definitely the minority. So, I think that will be an obstacle—just staying mentally strong.

We often heard a voice of resistance in girls' narratives asserting that they would "prove them wrong." They would fight unfair expectations and stereotypes about girls' and women's abilities by excelling in their chosen fields. Girls described their awareness of other people's assumptions and beliefs about the career paths they were choosing, as well as barriers they might face because of their gender. They described how they would become successful within their chosen field and that would be an enactment of their resistance. While it is true that the participants were aware of barriers and obstacles related to being women pursuing their chosen career and educational paths, they also, for the most part, indicated support from their families, friends, and in school. Though this sense of support is beneficial, it is essential to note that barriers and obstacles related to gender continue to exist even once one has attained a non-traditional career goal and is working in the field. For example, while there have been slight increases in women going into the military, women also leave the military prior to retirement at much higher rates than men for reasons related to "family planning, sexual assault, and dependent care" (Myers, 2020). While we might be setting girls up for success in achieving entry into STEAM (Science, Technology, Engineering, Arts, Math), and traditionally male-dominated career options, questions remain as to the level of support and acknowledgment of the complexity involved in long-term career success and satisfaction.

Challenging Stereotypes through Gender Identity and Presentation

Girls challenge traditional gender role stereotypes in their gender identity, expression, and presentation. Some of the girls we interviewed described their decisions to engage in activities deemed non-traditional for girls—be it sports or career choice. Girls resist cultural and interpersonal pressures to limit their choices of activities and demonstrate to others that these limitations should not be in place. Girls also challenged gender stereotypes about how they are expected to present themselves to others—through their outward appearance and behaviors.

Resistance can take the form of refusing to be limited to particular styles of gender presentation, such as attire and hairstyles, as well as attitudes and interaction styles with others. Girls demonstrate their resistance by refusing to be placed into one "box." A girl might enjoy getting dirty and playing sports and wearing frilly dresses and makeup. When asked what they like about themselves, the girls in our study listed many characteristics: intelligence, strength, independence, assertiveness, and relationality. They did not box themselves into narrow ways of being dictated by traditional gender roles. Girls in our studies recognized that endorsing traits that are not stereotypically feminine sometimes required resistance to social pressure. This resistance was often met with reactions and criticism from their peers. Ava (8th grade) said, "If it's a girl trying to act like a guy—not trying, but acting like a guy, they might think that she's trying to be tough."

Our research studies were inclusive of students who identified as transgender or gender non-conforming. Although not the focus of either of our studies, we acknowledge the importance of this literature as contributing to conversations about gender identity and resistance to traditional gender role stereotypes. A growing body of literature explores children's gender identity, including supporting children who identify as transgender or gender nonconforming in schools (Bochicchio et al., 2019; Goodrich and Barnaryd, 2019; Martino et al., 2020).

Direct Expressions of Resistance

Girls experience a range of interpersonal sexism, including sexual harassment, derogatory and demeaning comments and behaviors, and incidents where someone is trying to enforce traditional gender role stereotypes. In our interviews, girls described ways they directly expressed resistance during incidents of interpersonal sexism. For example, Alyssa (6th grade) described how she responded to sexism from her male peers: "I told them that it was very inappropriate, and I told them to stop and [that] next time, I would tell a teacher or a principal." Some of the girls described that they regularly engaged in direct resistance to experiences of interpersonal sexism. Ava (12th grade) said, "I'm usually pretty good at standing up for myself. I really don't let people walk all over me. I just say, like, 'Hey, yo, that's rude. Don't talk to me like that." For some girls, speaking out against sexism is part of their identity. They describe themselves as the type of person who actively expresses their disagreement with situations they think are wrong. Others begin to anticipate that they will speak out. For example, Tina (12th grade) shared:

> When I'm looking at them, they know, like, "Oh she is going to say something." I mean, I definitely speak out about it. I feel like if something isn't right, I'll definitely speak out about it. I don't just sit there silently.

While many of these interpersonal interactions occur face-to-face, girls also talked about experiences that took place online. Olivia (12th grade) described how she speaks up on social media when people say sexist things:

> I've always been really vocal about my opinion, and I've always had feminist opinions. And so, most of my family is [in] Texas, and they have their own opinion of what a woman needs to be, and I don't fit into that. I've always been really vocal on social media regarding my family about my opinion, and also if I see something—someone talking about someone on Facebook or Instagram … and it's sexist, I'm gonna say something about it.

Girls also described some of the reactions they received when they spoke up assertively about sexism. Kathleen (6th grade) talked about a time she was called a "slut" by her classmates and that they became more aggressive when she responded assertively to them:

> One time … my friend and I were at a football game, and some of the kids from my class called me a slut, and then they called me a bitch after that 'cause I was yelling at them.

Erin (11th grade) shared that she feels like people don't always take her concerns seriously:

> I feel when I speak up about it, it would be something like, "Oh, she's just being sassy," or, "She's being a bitch." 'Cause I feel like when girls ever want to speak their minds, they're seen as being too over the top, like, "How could you do that?" When a guy is speaking up for themselves, they're seen like, "Oh wow, he's a powerful guy."

Barriers to Resistance

Girls do not always engage in resistance to sexism, even when they want to. They might choose a less assertive response than they desire or decide not to respond directly. This is understandable given the many potential barriers to using a direct assertive response during sexist incidents. For example, in research examining children's intended responses to gender-based bullying, they reported a number of barriers to assertive responses including their emotional responses to the event (e.g., feeling nervous), circumstantial or setting limitations (e.g., not enough time to respond), social norms against being assertive, an authority figure stopping them, worrying about getting in trouble, or worrying about retaliation from the perpetrator (Brinkman and Manning, 2016)

Girls in our interviews explained that they make decisions about when and how to engage in direct forms of resistance based on the situation. For example, Eve (12th grade) talked about how she responds when she experiences street harassment and why she uses different approaches with boys her age and adult men:

> I'm like, "What just happened?" And then, if it's a teen boy, they'll be like, "Oh yeah," and I'll just kind of be like, "No," and I just slowly back away, almost, because I don't know what they're going to do. The few times it has been more adult men, I'm almost the exact opposite in that I suddenly get very angry because I'm just kinda like, "What the fuck are you doing? Get off of me," or something like that. And I—at least in my experience, if I do that to more teen boys, they're more willing to kind of fight me—physically—on it, and adult males are more like, "I don't want to cause a scene. I'll just walk away."

This disturbing example highlights how girls choose their responses based on their understanding of what will be effective in ending the situation and what might prevent the situation from escalating further.

There are also times when girls want to speak out about an experience and choose not to for various reasons. Nora (12th grade) described being frustrated when teachers asked for help moving things in the classroom and assumed that they needed boys to do it. When asked how she responds when this happens, she shared what she *wants* to say and what keeps her from saying it:

> I think it would just be like saying something like, you know, when they say … "I'll go get some boys," I can say well, you know, "I can do it" or, [think to myself] "Why don't I try?" But I don't really know what holds me back. Maybe … I don't know. Because I used to be one who would speak my mind, and I've kind of changed. I'm kind of willing to stand up for things, but I don't know, maybe just fear or the consequences or people not really understanding [holds me back]. That makes me frustrated because I feel a certain way, then you express that, and it's not understood. So, I don't know, something like that.

Resistance in Systems

In this chapter, we've outlined a body of research about how women and girls engage in resistance to sexism, and described the strategies utilized by girls in our studies. Even as we recognize the importance of this work, we want to avoid assumptions that resistance is simple or uncomplicated. In fact, resistance is occurring within contexts that are often repressing resistance and make resistance unsafe. We applaud girls for resisting and know we need to draw attention to the complex worlds they navigate. Drawing on Bronfenbrenner's (1979) ecological systems theory, Brinkman (2016, p. 40) explained how anti-bullying work needs to examine how different levels of interaction can impact bullying. A similar framework is essential for understanding girls' experiences of oppression. The microsystem of school climate is situated in the larger context of the community where the school is located, which is saturated in social and political messages. Importantly, the influence is bidirectional in that children and families are impacted while also impacting the larger systems.

As researchers, we can develop categories to understand resistance strategies, but to explore how these make sense in the real world we have to see the contexts in which girls live. In the next two chapters, we continue our exploration of resistance in context, focusing on masculinity (Chapter 5) and the sexualization of girls in schools (Chapter 6). Girls' resistance can build into efforts to create change in individuals and ultimately transform these systems.

References

Bem, S. L. (1993). *The lenses of gender: transforming the debate on sexual inequality*. Yale University Press.

Bergman, M., Langhout, R.D.Palmieri, P.A., Cortina, L.M. and Fitzgerald, L.F. (2002). The (un)reasonableness of reporting: antecedents and consequences of reporting sexual harassment. *Journal of Applied Psychology*, 87, 230–242. doi:10.1037/0021-9010.87.2.230.

Blum, R.W., Mmari, K., and Moreau, C. (2017). It begins at 10: How gender expectations shape early adolescence around the world. *Journal of Adolescent Health*, 61(4), S3–S4. doi:10.1016/j.jadohealth.2017.07.009.

Bochicchio, V. et al. (2019). Pre-service teachers' approaches to gender-nonconforming children in preschool and primary school: Clinical and educational implications. *Journal of Gay & Lesbian Mental Health*, 23(2), 117–144. doi:10.1080/19359705.2019.1565791.

Bosow, S.A. (2006). *Gender Role and Gender Identity Development.* In Worrel, J. and Goodheart, C.D. (Eds) *Handbook of Girls' and Women's Psychological Health.* Oxford University Press (pp. 42–251).

Brinkman, B.G. (2016) *Detection and prevention of identity-based bullying: social justice perspectives.* Routledge.

Brinkman, B.G., Goodkind, S., Elliott, K., Joseph, A., and Doswell, W.M. (2019). *Advocating for equity for Black girls: The formation of the Black Girls Equity Alliance.* A report commissioned by the Gwendolyn J. Elliott Institute.

Brinkman, B.G., Jedinak, A., Rosén, L.A., and Zimmerman, T.S. (2010). Teaching children fairness, decreasing gender prejudice amongst 5th graders. *Analyses of Social Issues and Public Policy*, 10, 171–191. doi:10.1111/j.1530-2415.2010.01222.x.

Brinkman, B.G. and Manning, L. (2016). Children's intended responses to gender-based bullying as targets and bystanders. *Childhood*, 23(2), 221–235. doi:10.1177/0907568215595095.

Brinkman, B.G., Rabenstein, K., Rosén, L., and Zimmerman, T. (2014) Children's gender identity development: A dynamic negotiation between conformity and authenticity. *Youth and Society*, 46, 835–852. Bronfenbrenner, U. (1979). *The ecology of human development: Experiments by nature and design.* Harvard University Press.

Brown, L.M. (2016). *Powered by girl: A field guide for supporting youth activists.* Beacon Press.

Brown, L.M., Chesney-Lind, M., and Stein, N. (2007). Patriarchy matters: Toward a gendered theory of teen violence and victimization. *Violence Against Women*, 13 (12), 1249–1273. doi:10.1177/1077801207310430.

Coltrane, S. (1998). *Gender and Families.* Pine Forge.

Curtin, N., Ward, L.M., Merriwether, A., and Caruthers, A. (2011). Femininity ideology and sexual health in young women: A focus on sexual knowledge, embodiment, and agency. *International Journal of Sexual Health*, 23(1), 48–62.

Dicke, A.L., Safavian, N., and Eccles, J.S. (2019). Traditional Gender Role Beliefs and Career Attainment in STEM: A Gendered Story?. *Frontiers in Psychology*, 10, 1053. doi:10.3389/fpsyg.2019.01053.

Eccles, J.S. (1987). Gender roles and women's achievement-related decisions. *Psychology of women Quarterly*, 11(2), 135–172.

Goodrich, K. and Barnard, J. (2019). Transgender and gender non-conforming students in schools: One school district's approach for creating safety and respect. *Sex Education*, 9(2), 212–225. doi:10.1080/14681811.2018.1490258.

Hinshaw, S. and Kranz, R. (2009). *The triple bind: Saving our teenage girls from today's pressures.* Ballantine Books.

Howe, K.G. (1985). The psychological impact of a women's studies course. *Women's Studies Quarterly*, 13, 23–24.

Impett, E.A., Schooler, D., and Tolman, D.L. (2006). To be seen and not heard: Femininity ideology and adolescent girls' sexual health. *Archives of Sexual Behavior*, 35(2), 129–142.

Klocker, N. (2007). An example of 'thin'agency: Child domestic workers in Tanzania. In *Global perspectives on rural childhood and youth* (pp. 100–111). Routledge.

Lawler, M. and Nixon, E. (2010). Body dissatisfaction among adolescent boys and girls: The effects of body mass, peer appearance culture and internalization of appearance ideals. *Journal of Youth and Adolescence*, 40(1), 59–71. http://link.springer.com/article/10.1007/s10964-009-9500-2.

Lytton, H. and Romney, D. (1991). Parents' differential socialization of boys and girls: A meta-analysis. *Psychological Bulletin*, 10, 167–196.

Magley, V.J. and Shupe, E.I. (2005). Self-labeling sexual harassment. *Sex Roles*, 53 (3–4), 173–189.

Magley, V.J., Hulin, C.L., Fitzgerald, L.F., and DeNardo, M. (1999). Outcomes of self-labeling sexual harassment. *The Journal of Applied Psychology*, 84(3), 390–402.

Mahalik, J.R., Morray, E.B., Coonerty-Femiano, A., Ludlow, L.H., Slattery, S.M., and Smiler, A. (2005). Development of the conformity to feminine norms inventory. *Sex Roles*, 52(7–8), 417–435. doi:10.1007/s11199-005-3709-7.

Mäkinen, M., Puukko-Viertomies, L.R., Lindberg, N., Siimes, M.A., and Aalberg, V. (2012). Body dissatisfaction and body mass in girls and boys transitioning from early to mid-adolescence: Additional role of self-esteem and eating habits. *BMC Psychiatry*, 12(1), 1–8. doi:10.1186/1471-244X-12-35.

Malkin, C. and Stake, J.E. (2004). Changes in attitudes and self-confidence in the women's and gender studies classroom: The role of teacher alliance and student cohesion. *Sex Roles*, 50(7), 455–468.

Martino, W., Kassen, J., and Omercajic, K. (2020). Supporting transgender students in schools: Beyond an individualist approach to trans inclusion in the education system. *Educational Review*, 1–20. doi:10.1080/00131911.2020.1829559.

Myers, M. (2020, May 20). The military needs a real plan to recruit and retain women, report finds. *Military Times*. www.militarytimes.com/news/your-military/2020/05/20/the-military-needs-a-real-plan-to-recruit-and-retain-women-report-finds/.

Norman, E. (Ed.) (2000). *Resiliency Enhancement: Putting the strengths perspective into social work practice*. Columbia University Press.

Orenstein, P. and Orenstein, P. (2011). *Cinderella ate my daughter*. HarperCollins.

Risman, B.J. (1998). *Gender vertigo: American families in transition*. Yale University Press.

Schaffer, D. (2000). *Social and Personality Development* (4th ed). Wadsworth.

Schoon, I. and Parsons, S. (2002). Teenage aspirations for future careers and occupational outcomes. *Journal of Vocational Behavior*, 60(2), 262–288. doi:10.1006/jvbe.2001.1867.

Sevelius, J. and Stake, J. (2003). The effects of prior attitudes and attitude importance on attitude change and class impact in women's and gender studies. *Journal of Applied Social Psychology*, 33, 2341–2353.

Shilo, M. (2021). Effects of television content on children's development of traditional gender role schemata: A literature review. *New York State Communication Association, 2017*.

Siegel, J.A. and Calogero, R.M. (2019). Conformity to feminine norms and self-objectification in self-identified feminist and non-feminist women. *Body Image*, 28, 115–118.

Stake, J.E. (2007). Predictors of change in feminist activism through women's and gender studies. *Sex Roles*, 57, 43–54.

Tolman, D.L. (2009). *Dilemmas of desire: Teenage girls talk about sexuality*. Harvard University Press.

Turner, S. Norman, E. and Zunz, S. (1995) Enhancing resiliency in girls and boys: A case for gender specific adolescent prevention programming. *The Journal of Primary Prevention*, 16(1), 25–38.

Watts, R.J., Diemer, M.A., and Voight, A.M. (2011). Critical consciousness: Current status and future directions. *New Directions in Child and Adolescent Development*, 2011(134), 43–57. doi:10.1002/cd.310.

Werner, E., & Smith, R. (1982). *Vulnerable but Invincible: A longitudinal study ofresilient children and youth*. McGraw Hill Book Company.

West. C. and Zimmerman, D. (1987). Doing gender. *Gender & Society*, 1, 125–151.

Chapter 5

Caution! Thin Ice

Navigating Fragile Masculinity

> *The girls won the state championship in basketball and the boys lost. If, you know, the boys' football team has won a championship and girls, you know ... had lost, they wouldn't even have acknowledged the girls in the assembly for the boys. But in the same assembly they acknowledged the girls' basketball teams, they also called up the boys' basketball team and acknowledged them for losing.*
>
> Mrs. Moore

To truly understand girls' resistance to oppression in schools, we must examine the contexts in which that resistance occurs. One factor we elucidate is how educational systems promote problematic expressions of masculinity and the way some boys behave within schools. In this chapter, we examine how toxic masculinity, White supremacy, and aggrieved entitlement of boys affected girls' experiences throughout their education. Rather than support boys in developing fortitude and resilience, schools frequently reinforce narratives of the broader culture that expect girls to take care of boys' feelings—even at the expense of their well-being. Boys' needs, desires, and challenges are consistently prioritized over those of girls in the schools. During our interviews, girls described situations in which they had to carefully navigate their interactions with boys in school—like skating on the thin ice of a reservoir of fragile masculinity.

Our data demonstrate numerous ways male entitlement was present in these schools, including the dangerous and toxic aggrieved masculinity displayed by angry White boys in the school. This entitlement spanned over a decade and impacted girls across all levels of education we studied (6th–12th grades) and was present in different schools. Girls utilized a range of resistance strategies to protect themselves in the context of these circumstances in their schools.

Prioritizing Boys' Sports

In our studies, schools often valued boys' participation in sports above that of girls. They also reinforced messages about the fragility of masculinity by

DOI: 10.4324/9781003111535-6

taking steps to protect boys' egos—such as the assembly described in the opening quote. While it could appear at first glance that schools celebrate the "strength" of masculinity as displayed through aggressive sports (football is often a prized activity) the narratives shared with us often focused on protecting boys—their egos, their educational opportunities, their focus, and their reputations. These narratives indicate that boys were often treated as if they were fragile and unable to handle disappointment, loss, competition (especially from girls), jealousy, or distress.

At Our Lady of Guadalupe Catholic High School, boys' sports were dominant, and male athletes were prioritized above others. Ms. Jackson shared, "When the girls' soccer team won state, they didn't have an assembly. They didn't really make a big deal out of it." Erin (11th grade) described the school's focus on boys' sports:

> Well, they do place a lot of emphasis on the guys' sports and stuff and not so much on the arts department. And so I feel like this whole school is centered around our football team and our sports teams and stuff like that—all of the coaches are in charge of everything, and everyone who is higher up status in the school is also a coach of something, of a men's team, so I feel like that gets priority.

Across both phases of our project, spanning over a decade in time, we heard accounts of how boys' sports were prioritized over girls' sports. Many of the 6th-grade girls in Phase One talked about being excluded by boys when they wanted to play sports. These incidents usually included a combination of forms of sexism—boys telling the girls they could not play with them, making derogatory comments about girls' ability to play sports, and then teasing the girls who wanted to play. Alyssa (6th grade) shared, "One time, I wanted to play football and they said, "No" because I was a girl. I felt pretty bad because I like football a lot, and I always play it with my cousins and everything … I thought I was really good at it." Ava described her repeated experiences in 6th grade trying to play sports with the boys, being left out, and feeling bad about how the boys treated her:

AVA: At Extended, which is like an after-school program, I always play softball with the boys. Well, lots of sports with them. And I'm always picked last because I'm a girl, and it makes me feel bad because I can be at least as good as everyone else in sports.

INTERVIEWER: Yeah. Do they say anything to make you feel like you're not as good?

AVA: Well, whenever I'm on a team, they always look disappointed that I'm on their team because they don't think I'm very good.

INTERVIEWER: Do they say anything about you being good, or do things change the next time you play? Or is it always that way?

AVA: Well, sometimes in soccer, if I made a goal or if I blocked a ball or something like that, then they say, "Good job." But I'm still picked last, like every time.

INTERVIEWER: And how does that make you feel?

AVA: It makes me feel left out.

This pattern of boys excluding the girls continued throughout middle school, even with some intervention from the school. The boys were told that they had to let girls play sports with them. However, as Ava shared during her interview the following year in 7th grade, this intervention did not necessarily lead to equitable or respectful treatment of the girls when they were playing sports:

> Last year, we really didn't have anything to do during recess. And so, me and a couple of my friends went to play football with the boys, and they would tell us what to do and everything, like, "Stand over there and block back a person." But they would never pass it to us, and whenever we wanted to play with them, they wouldn't pass or anything. They would just sort of let us play but exclude us.

This trend related to gender inequity in sports emerged again in Phase Two, more than a decade later. Girls and educators described how boys' sports were favored over girls'. Some of the preferential treatment appeared to be blatant and explicit, and some was more subtle. When asked if girls are treated differently from the boys in the school, Mr. Hill responded that boys' accomplishments in sports are celebrated more. He shared his perception that this is an artifact of a broader societal valuing of boys' and men's sports over girls' and women's sports:

> More people pay to go see the football game or the boys' basketball and say the volleyball games, you know. It's not something that is—I don't feel that starts just with the school ... this is the way it is. It's tough because we have a really great girls' basketball team.

Although Mr. Hill did not perceive this to be fair and just, per se, his narrative indicated that he saw this as a problem emerging outside the school. However, this perspective neglects to recognize that schools reinforce such inequities of sports between boys and girls in earlier grades and miss opportunities to disrupt societal messaging about boys' and girls' sports.

The educators we interviewed who worked in high often treated the devaluing of girls' sports relative to boys' sports as inevitable. Several perceived that their schools could not do anything to prevent this trend. However, as our data shows, many girls were interested in sports during middle school and were denied opportunities to play. When girls are consistently excluded, teased, and have to advocate for their rights to play, they will not get the same opportunities to improve their skills or be coached. Girls might also decide that it is not worth it to engage in sports if boys are excluding and teasing them and there is a lack of effective intervention from adults. Schools have opportunities in elementary and middle school to create the conditions for equity. When they do not do so, this reinforces the implicit message that boys are better at or more interested in sports than are girls. Any differentiation in sports between girls and boys in high school, college, and beyond might be directly related to experiences of sexism and exclusion in elementary and middle school.

Fragile Masculinity

Students and educators described preferential treatment of the boys' sports teams at Our Lady of Guadalupe Catholic High School. The boys' teams were celebrated for their effort even when they lost. In contrast, girls' sports teams were offered little fanfare and celebration. Numerous participants raised a specific incident as an example—an assembly where the boys were praised for losing—as described in the opening quote of this chapter. Nora (12th grade) talked about how the school consistently centered boys' accomplishments—even when those accomplishments were less significant than the girls':

> I think if boys do something significantly big then there's a lot of acknowledgment of that. Whereas, if girls do it, there is acknowledgment, but it may not be to the same level. Actually, it made me think when basketball—when boys' basketball took second place and then girls' basketball got state ... to recognize them, they had both teams stand up and just applaud equally. I was like, "The girls worked so hard. They took state. They should be recognized separately." So, that was frustrating. That did frustrate me because they deserved that. Not that we shouldn't recognize the boys for the good work that they did. But, you know, there should be a little something extra. And it's a huge deal. And there wasn't very much—and always for football and boys' teams, there's huge celebrations or whatever. But for, you know, for girls' basketball, there was like, "Okay, stand up for a few seconds," and that was it.

In addition to describing the school's culture emphasizing boys' sports, this incident highlights one of the ways the school reinforced *fragile masculinity*. Fragile masculinity describes the anxiety that boys and men might experience if they feel they are falling short of the cultural standards of masculinity (DiMuccio and Knowles, 2020). Erin (11th grade) described her reaction to these events, "The girls won, and they're placing so much emphasis on how well the guys did, and 'It's ok,' like, '*you don't have to win everything* [emphasis added].'" The assembly reassuring the boys' basketball team that they did a good job, even though they lost, was how the school system placated fragile masculinity. It was as though educators in the school were sending the message, "Don't worry, boys. Even though you lost, and the girls won, you are still masculine."

A growing body of research explores how manhood is experienced as a precarious state that one must attain and maintain. The theory of precarious manhood (Vandello and Bosson, 2013) suggests there are three core elements. First, manhood is viewed as a status that one must earn. This is reflected in common cultural statements like, "man up" or "be a man." Second, according to this theory, even if one successfully achieves manhood, it is impermanent, and the status can be lost or taken away at any time. Third, manhood is confirmed by others and requires public demonstrations. Men might experience anxiety about their masculinity's precariousness and engage in aggression, anti-femininity, and risk-taking to demonstrate their manhood to others. According to Crystal Jackson of the Good Men's Project, there are common symptoms and indicators of fragile masculinity, including men declaring "not all men" when one man is accused of misbehavior or asserting "men too" when discussing women's experiences of gender-based violence or abuse. Fragile masculinity can include feeling offended on behalf of oneself or other men, coming to the aid of unknown men without all the facts, or attempting to play devil's advocate in situations where men are under scrutiny. Accusing others of being sexist against men, or anti-male, can also be an indicator of fragile masculinity. Finally, displaying discomfort with being identified as a member of the LGBTQ+ community, being seen as feminine in any way, or making unnecessary efforts to clarify that one is not 1) feminine or 2) gay, are also displays of fragile masculinity.

For many boys and men, the pressure to achieve and maintain their manhood status creates anxiety that they try to relieve by engaging in compensatory behaviors, most often extreme examples of masculinity. Studies that have exposed men to masculinity threats have observed a range of reactions to the anxiety produced including aggressive ideation, anger, higher physiological stress responses, increased justification of social inequality, less support for gender equality, increased benevolent sexism, rejection of feminine activities, and being more aggressive toward gay men (see DiMuccio and Knowles, 2020 for a review of this literature). Through experiments, these studies demonstrate what many girls and women (and other boys and men) know from life experience. Fragile masculinity can lead to threats to other people—most often girls, women, people of color, and members of the LGBTQ community.

Girls in our interviews described how they navigated the potential threat of triggering fragile masculinity. This theme repeatedly emerged in conversations about girls being more intelligent than their male romantic partners. As we describe in Chapter 2, cultural acceptance for Smart Girls has increased over time, especially if the girls meet other expectations to excel and be Super. Even as girls and educators described this acceptance, there was a frequent caveat. Girls can be smart—but it becomes a problem if they are seen as more intelligent than boys, particularly if they want a romantic relationship with that boy.

INTERVIEWER: Well, what do you think happens if a girl is smarter than a boy ... especially, like, a boy she is dating or wants to date?

SLOAN: I don't know. At that point, I might feel like it's a barrier or something. Like, "Oh, she is too smart for me!" [Something like] that, [which] I don't think that matters very much.

INTERVIEWER: Uh-huh. Yeah. So, maybe the boy might worry or get insecure about it?

SLOAN: Yeah. He might, like, feel stupid, [or] dumb or something.

During Phase One of our project, girls talked about feeling pressure to choose between being open about their academic strengths and being accepted socially. They shared that being too intelligent could pose a barrier to heterosexual relationships. The barrier is fragile masculinity—boys feel threatened by dating a smarter girl. Girls navigated this challenge in different ways. Some engaged in direct resistance, refusing to do anything less than their best in school, even if this meant risking social ostracism. Some girls described how they and other girls would attempt to tiptoe around boys' insecurities in this realm by trying not to trigger their insecurities. They talked about watching their peers "dumb down" or act unintelligent as a form of flirting. Sloan (11th grade) said that girls downplay their intelligence "because they probably don't want to seem too smart, that ... like, the boy might just not be attracted to them." Some girls took up the strategy of modulating their own accomplishments to avoid triggering fragile masculinity in boys and the potential consequences to them and their relationships with those boys. Erin (11th grade) described how this strategy might play out in a heterosexual romantic relationship: "I also think girls would tend to downplay their smartness. If she's comparing her test to her boyfriend's, she's like, 'Oh, sorry I got a better score than you did.'" Girls have been given the message it is their responsibility to take care of boys' feelings, to avoid upsetting them, to avoid emasculating them. We heard girls describing this emotional labor that they engaged in within heterosexual relationships. This strategy of downplaying one's intelligence to protect boys' feelings was a theme in both phases of our study and a challenge that persisted over time.

Some of the girls in our studies talked about the adverse consequences they saw with employing this strategy. If girls frequently downplayed their intelligence for boys' sake, they might undermine their potential for learning and future success in their academic and career endeavors. Isabell (12th grade) described how this strategy could become internalized and lead to a pattern of self-doubt:

> I think it's unconsciously—you dumb yourself down enough to where you're acting dumb, but then it just becomes an innate behavior. And then you just learn this behavior, and it becomes a part of you. And it becomes a cycle of the girls belittling themselves for guys, and it just becomes a disaster.

While minimizing ones' academic strengths could protect social relationships in the short term and prevent the adverse outcomes of triggering fragile masculinity, it could also undermine girls' futures. Erin (11th grade) said this behavior "prevents girls from doing what they are really good at. Girls aren't seen as much in science and engineering and all of the STEM stuff ... basically being constantly told that they're not as smart or they're not as good." Eve (12th grade) also talked about the potential impacts on girls if they downplay their intelligence to avoid intimidating boys:

> It not only gives them a negative light of school 'cause that's obviously not like—we're here to learn stuff. Not necessarily that high school is the most important stuff you'll ever learn. But it's to get you interested. "What do you want to learn before going into college?" and when they're doing that, they're just coming off as–I know a girl who is the stereotypical kind of rich girl, wears high heels a lot, and I went to grade school with her when we were younger. She's a very smart, bright girl. At one point, she actually tutored people in math. She's a bright girl. But now, I see her and she's like, "How do you spell 'school' again?" And I'm like, "One—no offense, but you're overdoing it. Two, no." Other people don't know that [about her]. Most of the time she'll play it really well. And it's because she really wants to fill that role, the pretty girl in school that all the guys want. And, to her, that means she can't really be smart.

Resistance to Male Entitlement

Girls are forced to contend with boys' sense of entitlement and anger when they do not get what they want. Kate Manne (2020) explores how male entitlement interacts with other systems (e.g., White supremacy, classism, homophobia) to create unjust outcomes for girls and women. In her work, she examines several areas in which privileged men are tacitly deemed entitled to "goods." These goods include material resources and power, authority, claims to knowledge, and nurturing and care provided by women. Manne argues that if women fail to give men these goods men believe they are owed, women face punishment or reprisal—from men or the structures in which women are embedded. This punishment often presents itself in the forms of misogyny—hostility directed at girls and women to police their behavior.

In 2004 during the first year of our intervention with girls at St. Bernadette Catholic School, we saw how this pattern unfolded. We worked with all of the girls in the 6th-grade class, providing them with workshops about sexism. We gave the girls journals to track their experiences and bring to discuss at later workshops. In the third workshop, we invited the girls to share entries from their journals. To our disgust, we learned that boys in the class had stolen some of the journals, torn them apart, and taunted the girls for participating in the program. One girl reported that a boy had stolen her journal and saw that she had written about him being sexist. He was upset that she wrote about him and destroyed her journal. The girls shared that they felt violated during these interactions and were afraid of the boys in their class. This interaction exemplifies fragile masculinity and the aggressive responses that boys and men sometimes engage in when questioned or challenged. (See Brinkman et al., 2011 for more details about backlash from the boys).

The boys in the 6th-grade class demonstrated that they felt a sense of entitlement to any opportunities or resources given to the girls. The boys claimed that it was unfair that the researchers brought the girls pizza, soda, and cookies during the workshops (which extended into their lunch hour). The boys teasing the girls and stealing their journals were forms of misogyny designed to punish the girls for receiving something that the boys did not. We held a meeting with the boys to discuss their questions and concerns about the program. At the end of the session, the consensus was that the boys wanted a similar program. We thought it would be constructive for the boys to participate in workshops about masculinity and sexism and set up an intervention and research study. Not one single boy from the school participated in the program, despite the fact they had asked us to develop it for them.

The sociopolitical context in 2004 included rhetoric in scholarship and popular press asserting that there was a "boy crisis" in education. The late 1990s and early 2000s were consumed with questions about how boys were faring in schools in the United States, the United Kingdom, and Australia. Many argued that boys were being disadvantaged in educational settings—some explicitly blamed feminism and the empowerment of girls. Foster and colleagues (2001) offer a comprehensive review of these debates and the flawed data used to support them. Numerous studies demonstrated that the idea that boys are suffering in school because of girls' success is a myth and not supported by evidence (see, for example, Husain and Millimet, 2009). Unfortunately, this rhetoric infiltrated many schools and likely influenced how educators viewed and interacted with boys. We argue that this myth that boys were being mistreated in schools led to *increased* entitlement on the part of boys. Further, we have seen how boys' entitlement combined with the narrative that boys are being shortchanged by schools morphed into boys' aggrieved entitlement (which we detail below) a decade later.

Wealth and Entitlement

Male entitlement intersects with other systems of privilege to create conditions in schools in which some boys are granted access to resources and expect preferential treatment. For example, a student's social class might influence how they are treated within the school system. At Our Lady of Guadalupe Catholic High School, students and educators discussed how differences in wealth played out for students regarding social dynamics and treatment by the school administration. As a private school, Our Lady of Guadalupe charges families tuition for students to attend. Some families receive scholarships or reduced tuition based on their financial needs. Other families are financially able to pay the total tuition price, and some even donate additional money. The result is what some educators referred to as the "haves and have-nots." Ms. Larsen commented, "[There are the] haves and the have-nots and cliques, and, you know, again, the school tries so hard. And through their strong traditions, they really have the ability to create more unity than most. But it's always divided on economics." While students and educators did not necessarily know the financial situation of any specific student or family, they often made assumptions about the students based on clues, including whether the student had their own car, what type of car they drove, the vacations the family went on, and which students threw parties in their homes. For example, Mr. Walker said:

> No student has, to my knowledge, directly said this to me, but I really think there's this perception that the people that are on the boys' and girls' lacrosse team[s] and the boys' football team, they're wealthy. That status symbol of like, "Oh, their family has a lot going on." All those sorts of things.

Students and educators described one layer of entitlement that accompanied such financial resources—popularity. While it was not the only factor that would make a student popular, it was a common trait among popular students.

Wealth also frequently resulted in entitlement to special treatment by educators and the school administration. The school relied on the funds they received from families paying full tuition and from donations, and thus the administration stressed the need to keep the donor parents happy. The resulting dynamic was that children of donor parents had more access to the administration. The girls we interviewed noted that wealthy students had more voice within the school. Eve (12th grade) remarked, "I think the overall school treats more wealthy families better." They also shared that wealthy students got away with breaking the school rules. In particular, wealthy White boys could break school rules repeatedly and receive warnings for their behavior but face few meaningful consequences. Rose (12th grade) described how this dynamic played out in the school:

ROSE: There's a family here who has, like, gotten away with a lot just because their parents have a lot of money and donate a lot of money—

INTERVIEWER: They donate?

ROSE: Yeah. And there's a lot of kids whose teachers won't say anything to them or mostly, like, the administrators won't say anything to them, because they know that their parents have power over the school, kind of. And, like, they're—I think they're afraid of dealing with the parents 'cause they're like, if they're rich, sometimes, they're snobby 'cause they [the administrators] know they [rich parents] have the money to take away, basically, from the school. So, it's like, those kids are definitely treated differently. And then also, the [school principal] knows they have a lot of power, so sometimes those kids won't get in trouble. Like we got yelled at last week for some … like some alcohol issue or whatever. And the kids with money who are usually the ones who host that kind of stuff, like, don't individually get in trouble even though they [administrators] know where the root of the problem is.

Mr. Baker described how the administration's focus on keeping parents happy could limit teachers' ability to intervene when students engage in problematic behaviors:

> And if that kid goes to their parent and a parent calls the office, you're basically on the chopping block. People have gotten fired here for less. No, not that I'm all that scared of that, but that is something, too, you have to figure into the equation.

Angry White Boys

Scholars have analyzed how male entitlement can explain violent behavior, including mass shootings and violence at political protests (Katz, 2018; Kimmel, 2017, among others). In particular, the feeling of aggrieved entitlement might be an impetus that leads some men (and boys) into violence. Kimmel and others argue that aggrieved entitlement can offer insight into the phenomenon of "angry White men." "Aggrieved entitlement is a gendered emotion, a fusion of that humiliating loss of manhood and the moral obligation and entitlement to get it back. And its gender is masculine" (Kalish and Kimmel, 2010, p. 454). This is a cultural phenomenon on display within the United States in the form of political protests and riots filled with hate speech, property destruction, and physical violence towards others. For example, in 2017, a group of White nationalists marched in Charlottesville in a "Unite the Right" rally. They claimed they were protesting the potential removal of a Robert E. Lee statue (Gillon, 2017). The group of (mostly men) protesters yelled anti-Semitic chants and used anti-Black slogans. The nationalists destroyed property, injured others, and one woman was killed when a protester drove his car into a crowd.

Such events highlight the danger of aggrieved entitlement—the toxic combination of White men who feel that they are entitled to resources, success, political power, and visibility (e.g., in the form of statues), and who believe they are wrongly denied these entitlements. Angry White men use violence to assert their argument that they are being mistreated in a nation that is becoming increasingly diverse. On January 6, 2021 (while we were in the process of writing this book), a group of rioters led an insurrection on the United States Capitol Building—fueled by rhetoric from Donald Trump making false claims that the presidential election was stolen from him. The rioters invaded the Capitol to attempt to overturn the election results. Many people were injured and several people died. One analysis showed that of over 400 rioters who had been arrested or charged, 93% were White and 86% were male (See Amanpour and Company, 2021).

The political dynamics present on the national stage in the United States in 2016 infiltrated Our Lady of Guadalupe Catholic High School in numerous explicit and implicit ways. The rhetoric of the Trump campaign and the aftereffects of his election in the fall of 2016 reverberated through the school. One White male student walked into Kandie Brinkman's class on a free dress day (a day when students could be out of uniform) wearing a confederate flag on his hat. Even on free dress days, students are not allowed to wear hats within the building. His peers vocalized their interpretation that his choice of headwear was meant to send an intentional message to the teachers and students in the class about his political beliefs. We believe he also intended to send a second message—he felt entitled to break the school dress code and was confident that he would not receive any substantial consequences.

Unfortunately, this student had good reason to believe that he would not get in trouble. The school had allowed students to form a group they named "The Patriots' Club" during the Trump campaign. They claimed the club was a veterans' group club. However, the club consisted predominantly of White male students who asserted a White nationalist agenda within the classroom. Students created hats reminiscent of Trump's MAGA hats and sweatshirts that read "Patriots' Club," which they were allowed to wear as part of the school uniform.

Girls in the school, especially Latina girls, faced the consequences of the aggrieved entitlement of the White boys. Many talked about how unsafe they felt in the school because students in the Patriots' Club would take over classroom discussions. Some of these students commented that they grew tired of arguing with the boys about these topics. Maria (12th grade) described how this affected the climate of the classroom:

> Oh, except with the whole Trump thing—that made it hard for, like, a lot of students to feel comfortable in the classroom ... There's, like, those people who don't understand immigration or, like, don't

> understand anything about Latinos or immigrants at all, so, that's, like, really offensive, like.

Latinx students described the harassment they received after Trump was elected. They were laughed at and told comments like, "What are you going to do now to not get deported?" Rose (12th grade) talked about how this conflict played out in the classroom:

> And, like, during the election I think is the only time where that's been an issue. Like, there were people who would openly in class say, like, how illegal immigration isn't okay. That's messed up, like all this stuff. And I'm like, "There's people in here who have parents who had to come here illegally. Like, how do you think … you're making them feel right now?"

The school's permissiveness about the Patriots' Club further legitimized these beliefs and fueled the fire of the angry White boys. In our interviews with girls and educators at Our Lady of Guadalupe, we frequently heard the phrase *The Administration*, which we came to realize was used to refer to the all-male, all-White administrative team, including the principal, assistant principal, deans, and others. Some students argued that the Patriots' Club was allowed because student members espoused values that aligned with (their perception of) what the principal believed. Maria (12th grade) described her concerns about the Patriots' Club and students making racist statements in class:

> Yeah, and then the [principal of the school] is for Trump. So, it's obvious he's not gonna be like—I don't know, I feel like they just didn't do a good enough job of handling that, 'cause it's like, I don't know. They [administration] didn't want us talking about politics and stuff. But at the same time, they should make sure a student isn't feeling uncomfortable in the class, instead of just being like, "I don't know." They just didn't do anything to solve it afterwards, which is damaging.

And Liberty for Some

Girls utilized a range of resistance strategies against the racism they experienced during this time. In our interviews, multiple girls shared with us one particular story of resistance. Rose (12th grade) told us what happened:

> Like, one girl—she … did morning announcements. And she was trying to make, like—she was trying to bring attention to, like, how there isn't … equality in the world, basically. And so, she did the Pledge, and you know how it ends in "and liberty for all"? She said, "And liberty for *some*." And she's … the president of our Diversity Club. One of the

> teachers who is her AP teacher is super, like—I don't know, believes in White rights, I guess. I don't know how to say it, but she's like, "I refuse to teach her anymore."

The Latina student who led the Pledge that morning also talked about this experience during her interview. Maria (12th grade) described why she decided to take this action and what it meant to her:

> After Trump got elected, obviously lots of people were upset, as was I, and the next morning someone had asked me to do prayer. And so, I, like thought—I wanted to do something. I felt helpless; I felt very sad. So, in my prayer, I said, "We should pray for all those marginalized who will be—will continue to be marginalized, and we should come together as a community for everyone." And then, I said the Our Father in Spanish, and then I did the Pledge. And the only thing that I changed, because I was talking about how not everyone is included—instead of saying, "Liberty for all," I said, "Liberty for some." And that really, like—it was very interesting because it was not well-received by [the dean]. [But] it was well received by a lot of students, and students would message me, and teachers [would] actually come up to me. I had, like, 5 or 6 teachers who were like, "That was really great of you. We really support you on that."

While Maria did receive some support, she described backlash she faced for this and other actions of the Diversity Club (related to immigration and the Black Lives Matter movement). In Chapter 7, we further examine the activism of Maria and other girls—how they worked to transform not only their school but also engaged in wide-scale societal changes.

Resistance: Not Falling Through the Ice

Girls engage in resistance strategies to navigate problematic masculinity throughout their educational careers. Resistance is demanding opportunities for participation—in sports and in the classroom. Resistance is finding pathways for interpersonal relationships with boys, despite pressures to minimize their accomplishments so boys do not feel intimidated or threatened. Resistance is speaking up and naming the sexism of their male peers. Resistance is making visible the marginalized students in the school—using the microphones and platforms available, even when it means risking rejection from peers and teachers. Resistance is girls skating on the thin ice of masculinity year after year and not falling through. It is graceful and strategic and incredibly difficult.

Throughout our book, we have worked to center the perspectives and narratives of girls—seeking to honor the nuances of their experiences of oppression within schools. And we argue that schools often socialize boys into toxic forms of masculinity, which has direct and indirect impacts on girls' lives. We agree that "an emancipatory research program for girls would take into account the many ways that boys enter the world as the preferred sex" (Chesney-Lind and Irwin, 2008; p. 123). Girls experience multiple reminders that schools are designed to center the needs of boys, yet girls resist. We detail in the next chapter how schools reinforce the sexualization of girls and create unsafe environments for them, all under the guise of protecting boys. In part three of the book, we describe methods of transforming school systems to become spaces where all students can thrive.

References

Amanpour and Company. (2021, May 6). Studies show Capitol rioters were majority White men [Video]. PBS. www.pbs.org/video/studies-show-capitol-rioters-were-majority-white-men-ryn3m2.

Brinkman, B.G., Brinkman, K.G., and Toomey, S. (2011). What to do about the boys? Advocating for system change when doing social justice work with girls. *Journal for Social Action in Counseling and Psychology*, 3, 53–70.

Chesney-Lind, M. and Irwin, K. (2008). *Beyond bad girls: Gender, violence and hype*. Routledge.

DiMuccio, S.H. and Knowles, E.D. (2020). The political significance of fragile masculinity. *Current Opinion in Behavioral Sciences*, 34, 25–28. doi:10.1016/j.cobeha.2019.11.010.

Foster, V., Kimmel, M., and Skelton, C. (2001). "What about the boys?" An overview of the debates. In W. Martino and B. Meyenn (Eds), *What about the boys? Issues of masculinity in schools* (pp. 1–23). Open University Press.

Gillon, S. (2017, August 29). Why are so many White men so angry? *The Washington Post*. www.washingtonpost.com/news/made-by-history/wp/2017/08/29/why-are-so-many-white-men-so-angry.

Husain, M. and Millimet, D. (2009). The mythical "boy crisis"? *Economics of Education Review*, 28(1), 38–48. doi:10.1016/j.econedurev.2007.11.002.

Kalish, R. and Kimmel, M. (2010). Suicide by mass murder: Masculinity, aggrieved entitlement, and rampage school shootings. *Health Sociology Review*, 19(4), 451–464. doi:10.5172/hesr.2010.19.4.451.

Katz, J. (2018, January 14). Are we witnessing a crisis in White male masculinity? *Newsweek*. www.newsweek.com/are-we-witnessing-crisis-white-male-masculinity-781048.

Kimmel, M. (2017, December 15). Trump's angry white men. *Chatham House*. www.chathamhouse.org/publications/the-world-today/2017-12/trumps-angry-white-men.

Manne, K. (2020). *Entitled: How male privilege hurts women*. The Crown Publishing Group.

Vandello, J.A. and Bosson, J.K. (2013). Hard won and easily lost: A review and synthesis of theory and research on precarious manhood. *Psychology of Men & Masculinity*, 14(2), 101.

Chapter 6

"Are My Skorts Distracting You?"

Girls' Resistance to Sexual Violence

> *For the past, like, 2 years, we've been able to wear skorts to school. And then, at one point, they took all the girls in the assembly and—the whole thing essentially was like, "You're wearing the skirts inappropriately and ... you're being a distraction." We wear tights and leggings underneath, but we were told that we were being a distraction and we were inhibiting—we were impeding the guys' schoolwork. And that actually happened, and all the girls at the school wrote emails and sent them, actually printed them out, and hand-delivered them to the dean.*
>
> Olivia, 12th grade

> *And we've heard rumors where they said this happened and they said we weren't allowed to talk about it, or the girl would get kicked out of the school. Then our school is like, "If there's a problem with a guy, we don't want the police involved. We don't want this involved. So, you're going to be quiet and pretend like it didn't happen, ok?"*
>
> Grace, 12th grade

> *And I think it's scary. Like, mostly it's just scary to, like, think that you're never safe. And I'm not safe in my educational institution. I'm not safe when I go out in the streets. Like, I'm—there's really nowhere in the world that is actually safe.*
>
> Joy, 12th grade

Sexual violence against girls and women is one form of misogyny—behaviors that function as mechanisms to control and punish women (Manne, 2017). In this chapter, we examine how schools reinforce the sexualization of girls and promote sexual violence, thus creating hazardous environments that suppress girls' resistance and impede their opportunities to thrive. We document how girls navigated sexualization and threats of sexual violence and the lack of effective intervention from educators and administrators. We argue that the policing of girls' bodies daily through the constant surveillance of compliance with dress codes and the threat of sexual violence are forms of social control and backlash against girls gaining power within society.

DOI: 10.4324/9781003111535-7

Sexualization of girls can include any or all of the following experiences: 1) when a girl's value is derived only from her sexual appeal or behavior, 2) when a girl is held to a standard that equates a narrow definition of physical attraction with being sexy, 3) when a girl is sexually objectified and viewed as an object for others, or 4) when sexuality is inappropriately imposed on a girl (Zurbriggen, et al., 2007). An extensive body of research documents the harmful impacts of the sexualization of girls on their cognitive functioning, physical and mental health, sexuality, and attitudes and behaviors (see the *APA Task Force Report on the Sexualization of Girls*, Zurbriggen, et al., 2007). Girls who experience sexualization by others might internalize these messages in the form of self-objectification and poor body image. We situate our work among feminist researchers who have examined sexual violence within schools, including how girls are sexualized (Renold and Ringrose, 2013), while also being policed (and policing each other) regarding their sexuality (Raby, 2012).

Schools are embedded within societies and thus are impacted by the cultural influences that sexualize girls and make sexual violence permissible. School systems cannot be neutral regarding these issues; they can either create climates that reinforce the sexualization of girls or combat it. The creation and implementation of policies related to dress codes and sexual harassment, messages given to students about sexuality, and the response (or lack thereof) to instances of sexual violence all provide girls with information about their school's climate. It is within this maze that girls must navigate being sexualized by others and in which they make decisions about what resistance strategies to implement.

In this chapter, we draw upon the experiences shared with us by high school students at Our Lady of Guadalupe Catholic High School in response to dress codes, sexual harassment, and sexual assault. By listening deeply to the girls' narratives, we gathered new insights into their experiences and challenged our own existing beliefs or assumptions.

Dress Codes

Girls described their use of resistance strategies in response to sexualization in school through the dress code and its enforcement. It is important to note we did not initially ask about the uniform code. However, when we asked girls to talk about a time they were treated differently or unfairly because of their gender, many students shared the example described in the opening quote of this chapter. The school called all the girls into an assembly and told them they would be required to wear tights under their skorts year-round. For a reader who might be unfamiliar, skorts are skirts with shorts sewn underneath. Several girls in our study spoke extensively about this change to the uniform policy, how it was enforced, and labeled the problematic ways the dress code sexualized girls. Joy (12th grade) described how the dress code targeted girls and undermined their educational experience.

> And I think that undervalues the girls' learning in this space. Like, they pull you out of class because you're not wearing tights. I also think that's just kind of ridiculous that putting a black fabric over legs makes legs exist less and, I think that it was clearly directed towards girls. It was an email that said, "Girls, you now have to wear tights 24/7," and it occurred because I guess, even though these are skorts, they said that they were too short.

At Our Lady of Guadalupe, the dress code policy was detailed, specific, and gendered. The school's written handbook policy outlined different dress codes for male and female students and offered no awareness of the needs of non-binary, transgender, or gender non-conforming students. Although the dress code technically applied to all students, it was not enforced equally. Mrs. Moore noted that the dress code policy was explicitly enforced in ways that differed for boys and girls in the school:

> I do feel like the dress code is kind of set up in a way that makes it really easy to call out girls about how they're dressed and leaves boys alone for the most part. Girls are in violation of it a lot more frequently than boys are.

Girls of color experience hyper-surveillance regarding dress code policies, being targeted more often for enforcement strategies and experiencing more severe discipline for dress code violations (*National Women's Law Center Report*, 2018). Maria (12th grade), a Latina student at Our Lady of Guadalupe shared that educators made references to "certain" girls with "different" bodies", which we suspect was coded language alluding to girls of color.

> At first, it was all rule-based. It was just like, we don't want to have people thinking it is inappropriate. We want to make sure there is safety and everything. But then, a particular administrator came up and started talking about how girls have different bodies and how certain girls shouldn't be able to wear stuff like that ... it made it sort of like it was their fault that for looking that way. And then [the administrator] just started kind of talking about respect and being like, "Well, if you want to gain respect, you have to hide certain things and be modest and stuff."

The National Women's Law Center published a report titled "Dress Coded II" which described how schools enforce dress code policies based on gender with different restrictions for male and female students. Among the schools that maintained dress code policies, the restrictions ranged from makeup to width of sleeves and policies restricting head wraps and coverings. The report found differential application of dress code policies at schools with a majority of Black students, where there are almost double the number of dress code restrictions and suspensions of girls. A recent review of dress code policies in North Carolina public schools found that the policies reinforce heteronormative White patriarchal norms (Edwards and Marshall, 2020).

Girls in our interviews expressed their resistance to the messages conveyed to them explicitly and implicitly through the dress code and the policing of their bodies. For example, Joy (12th grade) challenged the idea that the school was promoting modesty as a value. She resisted the message that her body is a distraction to the boys:

> And they directly said—they were like, "We want to maintain a more modest look." And I think that, to say that modesty … even exists [laughs] is kind of flawed. And I think … that women are the ones that hold the burden for modesty, and women hold the burden for being the distraction and being the ones creating the problem when I think the problem is the male perception. Our male dean of students telling us that I—we as, like, some thirteen- and twelve-year-old girls that are starting at this high school are like somehow—clearly, like, the inferred … dialogue is that, "You—your body—is a distraction to the men that are supposed to be learning here."

The rhetoric of modesty being used as justification to be more restrictive about girls' attire starts well before high school. Ms. Jones, a middle school educator, described her experiences on a uniform committee at her school:

> And I was recently on … a uniform committee to add a couple kids on it, including one middle schooler. People were frustrated by the gendered roles. I'm trying to think of … other times. I think like if we do have … you know, a free dress day or something like that, they do feel like more restrictions are placed on what the girls can wear and what the boys can wear. It's much—there's much more of a concern about … keeping the girls quote un-quote "modest" and yeah.

Joy and other girls we interviewed resisted this language of modesty and challenged the policing of girls' bodies as a measure to protect boys from distraction. Whitman (2020) points out that many dress code policies contribute to the objectification of girls and the assumption that boys are incapable of controlling their desires. These dress codes construct girls' bodies as dangerous and a potential distraction to boys. Such policies claim to decrease or prevent sexual violence by targeting girls' bodies as problematic, sending the message that girls are objects and boys lack self-control or accountability. They reinforce myths that the way girls dress and behave is based on their attempts to be sexual *objects*—while discounting girls' rights to be sexual subjects and their right to an education free from objectification. Such dress code policies often include specific forms of policing girls and disciplinary outcomes.

Of particular concern to us was the description of the implementation of the policy, which involved directly modeling the evaluation and assessment of girls' bodies. Maria (12th grade) talked about one such "demonstration" and how degrading it was to her and other girls in the class:

> One of the teachers here used to grab a ruler and make all the girls—in front of the boys in the classroom—line up in the middle, measure each person's individual skirt, and if it wasn't fitting, you would have to go down to the office. I did that a couple times, and it's just like, I don't know—I feel like if it was too short you could just pull someone aside after class and be like, "Hey, can I talk to you?" and say "You should go down to the uniform store or go home." I think they could have handled it in a better way, in a way where it's not, like, degrading to the girls.

The policing of dress code policies also included explicitly sexual comments. Grace (12th grade) described her interaction with the dean and how it made her feel:

> [T]he first thing was, we were supposed to wear tights with our shorts. Not a big request. It's winter; that's totally fine. So, I come to school in sheer tights, and I get told by our dean that I can't wear those because I look like a Victoria's Secret Model. And I remember that comment being like—and me and the dean are very close. He's my track coach, and it wasn't so weird that I was like, "What the heck?" I remember I thought that was a very interesting way to phrase that, obviously ... So, I switched to darktights.

As the girls we interviewed clearly articulated, the impact of such sexualizing dress codes is harmful to girls. Dress code enforcement that results in girls being asked to leave the room to get "shame clothing," sent to in-school suspension, or sent home to change clothes directly results in lost educational time for girls. The claim that these dress codes are designed to protect boys' education by "freeing" them from distraction does not consider the harm to girls' education. When dress code enforcement also includes statements about girls' bodies and visual demonstrations of how to objectify girls, they are also teaching students how to sexually objectify girls, while also making girls feel unsafe in their schools. Olivia (12th grade) shares her thoughts on this:

INTERVIEWER: What kind of message is it sending to both female and male students? Do you think that to be like the girls, you have to wear different clothing because it's distracting male teachers and male students?

OLIVIA: I think it just says that you are going to be sexualized, like, at whatever age you are, even if you are just a high schooler. And it's really sad, and it sends the message that "Guys, it doesn't really matter what you wear—and girls, you have to be constantly conscious about what you look like and your appearance." Whether you're dressed modestly or whether you look a certain way that fits a standard.

INTERVIEWER: And to protect them from boys or their feelings or something.

OLIVIA: It's like an insult to the guys too. It's like saying, "Oh, they can't control themselves," or something like that, and that's a lie. [Laughter] It's a lie.

Many of the girls articulated during the interviews that they had concerns about the policy: that it was unfair to girls, that it sexualized girls, that it was enforced in problematic ways that lead the girls to feel unsafe. The girls described a formal protest they formed in response to the dress code policy, which we detail in Chapter 7. Unfortunately, many K-12 schools have dress codes that reinforce sexualizing messages and school cultures (Harbach, 2015). We argue that the growing trend of dress codes that explicitly sexualize girls (naming their clothing as provocative)—and dress code enforcement that disproportionately targets girls, gender non-conforming students, and Black, Indigenous, and people of color students—is a form of backlash against the movements which have empowered girls.

Sexual Harassment

As we described above, many of the students opened their interviews by sharing their concerns about the dress code and policing of girls' bodies. The students conveyed passionate resistance to the messages telling girls their educational needs were secondary to those of the boys and challenged dangerous cultural messages that boys are not responsible for their behavior. As the interviews continued and we asked the students directly about sexual harassment, we found that the narratives of resistance became less confident. Girls questioned their experiences but also articulated some feelings of helplessness. They described the lack of effective intervention from educators and administrators and how this affected their decision about how to resist these experiences.

According to numerous studies, sexual harassment is a severe and pervasive problem in K-12 schools in the United States and throughout the world (see Brinkman, 2016 for a review). A landmark American Association of University Women study conducted with students in grades 7–12 found that 56% of girls reported being sexually harassed at school (Hill & Kearl, 2011). Within the context of the #metoo movement, additional large-scale studies were commissioned with the goal of understanding the scope of sexual harassment within the United States. In one such study, 57% of women reported experiencing sexual harassment by the age of 17 (Kearl, 2018). Sexual harassment in school can take many forms, including unwanted sexual comments and gestures, unwanted touching, being flashed, the spreading of sexual rumors, receiving unwanted sexual pictures, and more (Brinkman et al., 2021). Tina (12th grade) shared her experiences of sexual harassment following the end of a romantic relationship:

> I did date this one boy, which was a bad idea in itself—and I knew it was a bad idea. And it ended badly. And he, of course, went around spreading all of these rumors. And I tried to be like, "That's not true, that's not true." But at that point, everyone was just saying it, so I was like whatever—I just don't care anymore. I just would say I didn't care, but like, I mean, of course it hurt.

Experiencing sexual harassment in school can lead to numerous emotional and physical adverse effects. Sexual harassment can also negatively impact girls' educational experiences, including increased tardiness, difficulty studying, missing school, or wanting to stay home from school to avoid being harassed (Brinkman et al., 2021; Strauss, 2012). Sexual harassment has more significant impacts on engagement in school and academic performance than bullying (Gruber and Fineran, 2007).

Given the demonstrated pervasiveness of sexual harassment and negative impacts of sexual harassment on girls' educational experiences, we should expect schools to prevent and appropriately respond to sexual harassment. Within the United States, federal legislation mandates that schools do just that. Title IX prohibits discrimination in schools based on students' sex or gender, and specific guidance is offered about how schools should address sexual harassment. Further, school policies, their implementation, and the messaging that surrounds them contribute to the culture and climate of a school, which impacts the rates of sexual harassment. Rinehart and Espelage (2016) found that when teachers perceive their schools as being committed to prevention, students report less sexual harassment perpetration and victimization. Another study of over 85,000 high school students found that when students had positive perceptions of their school climate, the negative impacts of sexual harassment decreased, suggesting that positive school culture can be a protective factor against the harms of sexual harassment (Crowly et al., 2021).

Strikingly, our study found that when educators were asked about sexual harassment policies and procedures in their schools, the responses were overwhelmingly vague. Many did not know if a policy existed or what it said. Some offered that they assumed there was language within the student handbook but were uncertain regarding specific details. Many educators also said they lacked confidence in how well the policies were implemented. Mr. Hill said, "Well, to be honest with you, I have to go back and read our policy in our handbook. But my feeling is that the letter of the law isn't always followed strictly." Mr. Walker noted that there was a policy about sexual harassment in the handbook and spoke to how he would respond but shared that he had little faith in the administration's response to his reports, saying, "Don't know what the school, then, ever does with it." Ms. Powell also indicated that she was unclear about how the administration would proceed in cases of sexual harassment.

INTERVIEWER: Can you ... generally judge, "Okay, if I responded this way, it's probably congruent with what the administration's going to do"? Or is that like a black box and you don't know?

MS. POWELL: I really have no idea. I just don't. I have a feeling for me, but I have a feeling that it varies depending on the people who are the people involved.

None of the educators could share in detail how the school defined sexual harassment, what steps were taken to educate students and prevent sexual harassment, or how to respond most effectively. We do not assume from our conversations with educators that the schools did not have sexual harassment policies. In fact, we assume that they do—either at the school level or the school district level. At some point in time, a lawyer probably crafted a policy to ensure that the district would comply with Title IX. However, a policy that no one knows serves no one. Further, Wilmot, Migliarini, and Ancy Annamma (2021) refer to the "double helix of oppression" (p. 362), operating to perpetuate the harm being done to Black girls in schools. Their analysis revealed problematic responses from educators to problematic school policies which combined to ignore, invalidate, and fail to protect students, particularly Black students, from sexual harassment.

In addition to lack of clarity about policies prohibiting sexual harassment, in our interviews with educators we heard narratives of victim-blaming and minimization of sexual violence and its impact on girls. This minimization took many forms, including the belief that girls are overreacting when they talk about sexual harassment. Ms. Powell said:

> A lot of being offended is manufactured because sometimes there are messages that they feel like they're supposed to be like one girl, you know. So, one girl said, "Okay, why do, you know—why do they say that?" And then somebody decided to make a crusade out of it. So, I don't know. I don't know what the school's policy is or if there even is one. I don't know. Well, okay. Yeah. Obviously, there was one [policy]: harassment is bad, you're going to get in trouble, that kind of thing. What gets into that is—that's what I don't really know because I feel like that line is different on the agenda.

Another educator talked about sexual harassment as problematic behavior but denied the gendered element of the experience. Mrs. Carter commented, "But there is a lot of harassment that goes on that's not appropriate. I think it's both ways." Rahimi and Liston (2009) described the connection between teachers failing to act on reports of gendered harassment and the teachers' beliefs about sexuality, race, and gender. Specifically, they found that middle school teachers who believed the sexuality of female students was a taboo topic, and sexuality and desire of male students was appropriate, were more likely to ignore female reports of sexual harassment. Even educators who did not engage in victim-blaming and who want to support students who experience sexual harassment will be limited by the training and support they receive from the administration.

We argue that the extensive time and energy spent policing the sexualizing dress code policies—in combination with the lack of attention to policies and procedures to prevent and respond to sexual harassment—sends a message to educators and girls. About whose needs in the school are being met. About what behaviors are problematic and what ones are acceptable. We argue that the lack of training about sexual harassment represses girls' resistance to sexual harassment. Given these conditions, it was not surprising that some girls in our study talked about sexual harassment with narratives that suggested they experienced learned helplessness. For girls experiencing sexual harassment this might take the form of reluctant acceptance of continued harassment. For example, Tina (12th grade) talked about giving up on resisting sexual harassment because she felt that speaking up about it would not be effective:

> We had this cute little astronaut costume, and it was really cute, super fun, and they called us "astro-sluts," like in the middle of the assembly just screaming it. And we were like, "That's cool," just taking it. And when it came to my senior year, I was captain, so I finally get to say stuff, but then I didn't want to at that point, because they aren't really going to care, so it doesn't matter.

Learned helplessness is a common reaction to stressors that are pervasive, personal, and perceived to be permanent. The sexualization of girls in this school fits all of these elements. The pervasiveness of sexualizing messages conveyed through dress code policing and sexual harassment from peers presented a daily threat. Teachers and administrators making specific and direct comments about a student's body is deeply personal. And the lack of policies or programs to prevent harassment would lead many girls to believe that these conditions will never change.

One potential pathway of resistance to sexual violence is asking an adult for help. It was notable that none of the students we interviewed talked about turning to adults for help or support regarding sexual harassment.

Girls will not report to educators or administrators if they believe that they won't be supported or that nothing will be done about the incidents. Girls in our study shared that they lacked faith that the school would respond to sexual violence because of their previous experiences with school administrators on this issue. For example, Nora (12th grade) said, "Because there's no point in coming to administration or saying anything because of my past experiences, I didn't have any hope that they would do anything. So, I didn't want to go and get let down." Nora's quote demonstrates that when girls experience sexual harassment repeatedly and the school does not respond in a supportive and effective manner, some girls will stop turning to the adults in the school for help. In their study of black, middle school girls, Harris and Kruger (2020) found that "It seemed teachers placed the onus of responsibility for sexual harassment on the girls rather than the other actors at the school, including school leaders and male peers." (p. 17). We argue that by refusing to address sexual harassment appropriately, the school is effectively suppressing one avenue of girls' resistance to this form of sexualized violence.

Sexual Violence

During our interviews with students and educators, we grew increasingly alarmed by what we learned about how schools responded (or did not respond) to sexual violence. When discussing sexual violence, girls' resistance most often took the form of distrust of the school—expressing that they knew the school would not protect or support them and they would be best positioned by not relying on them to do so. The threat of sexual violence in the school—and the lack of trust that the school will address sexual assault appropriately—created a feeling of being unsafe in a place the girls had to attend daily. For some students, this likely triggered survival dissonance.

Many of our interviewees raised one specific incident—a girl was sexually assaulted while on a study abroad trip with the school. At the time of the interviews, there was a pending lawsuit against the school about the case. When asked about what the school does to manage "locker room talk," Rebecca (12th grade) talked extensively about the incident, and her feelings about how the school responded:

REBECCA: I think if an issue comes up, they try to cover it up because—well, I don't know if you know, but we recently had something happen … and I don't know, like, the true story, but one girl claims she got raped while on vacation with us as a school over in Germany. And that teacher [who chaperoned us] is no longer here. But [the rapist was] just some foreigner that had broke [*sic*] into their room, and the teacher didn't know. And then, they just flew home the next day, and she [the victim] said the teacher said, "Well, this kind of stuff happens all the time." And it was a woman teacher too, so I kind of know who it is without disclosing any names. But she—and they couldn't fire her because of some contract reason, but she resigned anyway. But I think right now because they're dealing with that lawsuit, it's kind of funny that—it's a little fishy to me that the parents and the student decide to sue now because we haven't gone overseas for two years so it's kind of fishy that—

INTERVIEWER: It didn't happen while it was all going on.

REBECCA: Yeah, it [lawsuit] happens now instead of when it [rape] happened. But, so, yeah, they kind of just covered that up and are covering that up right now to act like nothing's happening. So, I don't think they, like, formally addressed it, and if they did, I think it would be the dean addressing it. I don't think it would be administration. Well, I guess he's part, but yeah.

INTERVIEWER: So, is there a sense of how this event has affected—because obviously, some people know more I'm sure, and some people know less. But [is there] sort of a perception that if the school's gonna cover up, you know, a girl being raped—do you feel like a lot of students have that same perception, that they think, well, that might happen or it will likely happen?

REBECCA: I feel as, in regards to, if they feel safe, I think we do. We have a very good—it's well-maintained, it's well-looked-over, like, we're very close with our teachers, but it's looked-over. And they make sure it's appropriate and all that. If—wait, can you say the question again?

INTERVIEWER: Yeah. I said it in this really confusing way. Do you have a sense that students worry? And, you know—

REBECCA: Oh, okay, sorry. But as far as the general consensus of how we perceive the school, I think all of us would say that if something happened, it would be covered up.

INTERVIEWER: So, you feel that mostly people feel that they're safe, but if something were to happen, then it might get covered up.

REBECCA: Yeah, and I think it would just get like—people would—it would just go away. But of course, it's like a problem that would always be there.

INTERVIEWER: Right. And what impact do you think that has on [how] the students' feel, like—whether it's true or not—like, maybe they would, but most students think they would make it go away. What impact do you think that has on students?

REBECCA: Well, for us who've kind of been here for many years care very much about loyalty. So, like, kind of when you become one of us, like, you just kind of go along with that. So, I feel we—since we feel like rules make us, and our contracts that we sign have to be bound to that, I would say we would just go along with it. But maybe for students who are looking to come in and heard about it, I think that would empower them more than us. If it wasn't so covered up, I think it would impact us more, especially depending on the way they dealt with it. If we just heard about it, and they didn't address it, and it was very well known, and they didn't try to cover it up so fast, we would probably be worried and have that kind of alertness or alarm. But since it is [covered up], it's not there. However, if that were to happen and they were to come out and take responsibility, I think that it would convey a different message if it was genuine.

INTERVIEWER: Do you think girls—if a girl ... did experience sexual violence from, you know, a classmate or a teacher, that sense that the school's going to cover up my—do you think it would affect how she would feel?

REBECCA: It might. Maybe that's why they waited so long if that's true. I would say yeah, maybe, but depending on how much it impacted you, and you would obviously need to address it.

Based on Rebecca's interview, we suspect she was experiencing survival dissonance (as we describe in Chapter 3), as she justified the school's decision to cover up the sexual assault during the study abroad trip. She offered that perhaps the school considered the students' needs by *not* telling them about the event. She also affirmed her sense of loyalty to the school and the school climate of not "causing trouble" that we heard about in other interviews. She asserted that most students feel safe while also positing that the school would cover up a sexual assault if it happened.

This excerpt also revealed how challenging these conversations were for us as interviewers. We were taken aback by what unfolded in the interviews. We had not anticipated the intensity of interviewees' reactions and experiences with the dress code situation. We were deeply disturbed when girls shared the story about the rape cover-up and their certainty that it would happen again. We sought to honor the girls' experiences, their hesitation, their fear, and their reluctance. As interviewers, we intended to hold the space to allow the girls to talk about their experiences without pushing them to share when they didn't feel safe or attempting to reconcile what we saw as contradictions.

One of the teachers, Mrs. Larsen, also talked about this incident during her interview:

> One of my girls was on a trip, and a security guard—but I wonder. I don't know to what extent girls are educated. Um, when they say "rape," do they understand the definition of rape, or is she really saying, "He touched my breasts?" I'm not sure what she told me. And then, we had to kind of look at legal reporting [to see] whether she was just backtracking. You know, it's hard to say, but there's just a part of me that wonders too ... that these kids are so sexual in their talk. And yet, you realize that there really is a lack of education.

Throughout the interview, Ms. Larsen described ways she supports girls and works to challenge sexism in the school (and elsewhere in her life). And yet, in her description of the sexual assault on the study abroad trip, she hesitates to believe the girl. She questions whether the victim truly understands what rape is. We read this also as the result of survival dissonance. It was challenging for us to make sense of the story of Mrs. Larsen, who is a long-term educator in the school and is explicitly devoted to feminist issues, yet accepts that the school would cover up sexual violence. It might have been easier for her to believe that the incident was not as serious as the girl said.

Despite the seeming expectation that they should be victims of sexual violence in their school, girls resisted acquiescence. They challenged how the school handled sexual violence. They asserted their concerns about the mistreatment of their peers. They affirmed that they were entitled to feel safe in their school. Grace (12th grade) described that she does not trust the school's administration to deal with sexual assault and that she would seek outside help if she were to experience sexual violence:

> And we've heard rumors where they said this [sexual assault] happened, and they said we weren't allowed to talk about it or the girl would get kicked out of the school. Like, so many, and you're like, "How much is this true and how much is not?" But if everything that is said about our administration is true and … if that much is said, then a couple of the pieces are [true]. They're not—that means our school is like, "If there's a problem with a guy, we don't want the police involved. We don't want this involved. So, you're going to be quiet and pretend like it didn't happen, ok? And we'll do this for you." And obviously, like, not all cases we've heard are true. But I feel like one or two are, and I feel like at that point—so, I know if I had a problem, I'd go to my parents and I'd go about it that way. I think my parents at this point are smart enough that we wouldn't—like, the school wouldn't do anything for us.

Students conveyed their resistance by recognizing they should not put their trust in the school. They also articulated that the school's approach reflected a sexist attitude that promoted toxic masculinity and protected boys at the expense of the safety of girls in the school. Joy describes her resistance to the school's approach to sexual violence and the way the school protects boys, especially football players. She also details the difficulty of maintaining resistance—how much energy it requires and being unsure of the outcome:

JOY (12TH GRADE): There's a very, like, "boys will be boys" kind of attitude here. Like, "If you're on the football team, it's fine [to commit sexual assault]" kind of thing. Like, they just recently had a lawsuit against them for covering up a rape case that happened on, like, a school trip. And I've, like, been hearing more about another case where a girl came into the administration to say she was raped, and they notified the boy before she could go to the authorities so that *he* could have more protection. And that's just really astonishing to me that, like—and it's not that I'm like, "Oh that's shocking that this can still happen," because, like ... it's very prevalent and, like, all you have to do is look for it.

INTERVIEWER: Well, it's not shocking, but how—how does it make you feel? Any of these examples?

JOY: I think that it's very disheartening to even—'cause, like, a lot of the time, you get pumped up by, like, the movement and ... it's, like, exciting to be a part of, like, kind of a revolutionary standpoint. And there's so many things like you can ... wear a shirt that says, "Girl power." Like I have a sticker on my laptop that says, "Cats against catcalls" and it's ... like, a nice way to, like, surround it. But then, like, when you actually think about, like, the way that you feel when you're catcalled, like the physical danger that, like, is created through the ideas that they're perpetuating, like .... By saying that women don't have the power to decide what they wear, and that men are incapable of [not] being ... distracted by something that girls have been wearing from the beginning of this school, furthers the ideas that men are incapable of controlling themselves from, having sex with a woman or that, like, they're incapable of ... teaching somebody a lesson. And, I think that it's just—it gives men an excuse to say that they're predisposed to have less control.

INTERVIEWER: Yeah. It's—and lowers expectations of what—

JOY: Yeah. Mm-hm. And I think it's scary. Like, mostly, it's just scary to, think that you're never safe. And I'm not safe in my educational institution. I'm not safe when I go out in the streets. Like, I'm—there's really nowhere in the world that, like, is actually ... safe.

INTERVIEWER: So, what do you do when these sorts of things happen? The tights, for example.

JOY: I think most of the time there's not a lot that you can do, and it's hard because—you're faced with like the dichotomy of are you going to, like, push against the system and possibly make it so that you don't have what you do have, or are you going to just, like, try and work with the system in the ways that are more beneficial to you? And I think that the second one kind of makes you feel like a sellout. It makes me feel like I'm like participating in the ... very system that oppresses me. But also, like, it's hard to know what else there is to do when nobody's going to care. And, so, it's hard to know what the point is 'cause I'm sure that, like ... Rosa Parks didn't know she was gonna start the Freedom Riders. I think it's difficult to know, which thing is going to work and which thing's gonna get you kicked out of high school, like [laughs].

Resistance Toward Liberation

We, the authors (three women), know all too well that there is not one ideal path for resisting sexual violence, but rather, girls must navigate each incident as it happens. Our intention in this chapter is to honor the voices of the girls who bravely shared their experiences with us. We held witness as girls talked about their resistance strategies and the harm they experienced from dress code enforcement. We also heard girls' frustrations with the response (or lack thereof) from administrators within the school. We talked to educators who were unable to clearly articulate their school's policies or responses to sexual harassment, creating doubts for us about whether they were well-equipped to support students who faced sexual harassment (and we suspect, leading the girls to question this as well). We also heard about administrators' permissiveness, justification, and reinforcement of boy's behaviors and denial of sexual violence. We held space for girls' experiences, their voices, their resistance, and their agency.

Adults can support girls in developing strategies of resistance for liberation, which serve to transform girls' lives and their environments. Liberatory resilience or resistance strategies "empower girls through the confirmation of positive self-conceptions as well as strengthening connections to the community" (Evans-Winters, 2005, p. 43). As girls use these resistance strategies, they participate in the process of transformation of self and community, which is the focus of the last section of this book. We believe such transformation is possible and necessary—girls deserve to attend institutions of education that are safe where they are free from violence and can learn, grow, and thrive.

References

Brinkman, B.G. *Detection and Prevention of Identity-Based Bullying: Social Justice Perspectives* (2016) Routledge Press.

Brinkman, B.G, Elliott, K., Bates, S.L., and Smith, O. (2021).Centering Black Girls in Sexual Harassment Research: A Community-Based Participatory Action Research Approach, *Women & Therapy*, doi:10.1080/02703149.2021.1961432.

Crowly, B.Z., Cornell, D., and Konold, T. (2021). School climate moderates the association between sexual harassment and student well-being. *School Mental Health*, 1–12. doi:10.1007/s12310-021-09449-3.

Edwards, T.K. and Marshall, C. (2020). Undressing policy: a critical analysis of North Carolina (USA) public school dress codes. *Gender and Education*, 32(6), 732–750.

Gruber, J.E. and Fineran, S. (2007). The impact of bullying and sexual harassment on middle and high school girls. *Violence Against Women*, 13(6), 627–643. doi:10.1177/1077801207301557.

Harbach, M.J. (2015). Sexualization, sex discrimination, and public school dress codes. *University of Richmond Law Review*, 50, 1039.

Harris, J. and Kruger, A. C. (2020). "We always tell them, but they don't do anything about it!" Middle school Black girls experiences with sexual harassment at an urban middle school. *Urban Education*, 1–27. doi:10.1177/0042085920959131.

Hill, C. and Kearl, H. (2011). *Crossing the line: Sexual Harassment at School.* American Association of University Women. www.aauw.org/resources/research/crossing-the-line-sexual-harassment-at-school.

Kearl, H. (2018). The facts behind the #metoo movement: A national study of sexual harassment and assault. Stop Street Harassment. https://stopstreetharassment.org/wp-content/uploads/2018/01/Full-Report-2018-National-Study-on-Sexual-Harassment-and-Assault.pdf.

Manne, K. (2017). *Down girl: The logic of misogyny.* Oxford University Press.

Raby, R. (2012). *School rules: Obedience, discipline, and elusive democracy.* University of Toronto Press.

Rahimi, R. and Liston, D.D. (2009). What does she expect when she dresses like that? Teacher interpretation of emerging adolescent female sexuality. *Educational Studies*, 45(6), 512–533.

Renold, E. and Ringrose, J. (2013). Feminisms re-figuring 'sexualisation', sexuality and 'the girl'. *Feminist Theory*, 14(3), 247–254.

Rinehart, S.J. and Espelage, D.L. (2016). A multilevel analysis of school climate, homophobic name-calling, and sexual harassment victimization/perpetration among middle school youth. *Psychology of Violence*, 6(2), 213–222. doi:10.1037/a0039095.

Whitman, G.M. (2020). A Curricular Critique of School Dress Codes. *The Clearing House: A Journal of Educational Strategies, Issues and Ideas*, 93(2), 72–77.

Wilmot J.M, Migliarini V., and Ancy Annamma, S. (2021), Policy as punishment and distraction: The double helix of racialized sexual harassment of Black girls. *Educational Policy*, 35(2), 347–367. doi:10.1177/0895904820984467.

Zurbriggen, E.L.et al. (2007). *Report of the APA task force on the sexualization of girls.* American Psychological Association. www.apa.org/pi/wpo/sexualization.html.

Chapter 7

Planting Seeds of Change through Girl-Led Activism

So, like, all the girls that were angry, knowing that I was kind of angry with them, came to me ... complaining and saying, "That's not fair. We just got them [the skorts}. It's not our fault that this is how it is." And so, I decided that all of us should write a letter to the administration telling them how we feel, how that felt sort of degrading, how they could have went about it a different way. So, about 50 of us girls wrote letters, [and] gave it [sic] to [the dean].

Maria, 12th grade

Well, dear reader, you made it. If your experience of reading this book is anything like our experience writing it, you may have found yourself feeling angry, frustrated, and even hopeless about the state of education. Over the decade that we studied girls' experiences to inform this book, we have seen some improvements in the conditions for girls, some aspects of education have remained stagnant, and some things have gotten worse. Being a girl in school in the USA (and likely many places around the world) is exhausting and hard work. It requires navigating a myriad of pressures to be perfect, to be compliant, to manage rowdy boys, to be assertive but not bossy. It means having your body policed so that others are not "distracted," being subjected to sexual harassment and violence, and being let down by educators and administrators who prioritize boys' reputations over girls' safety. Girls must also face the additional challenges posed by racism, classism, and homophobia. Oh, and in the meantime, try to get an education.

Despite all of these challenges, girls fight for themselves and for better schools. There are educators who hold witness to the struggles girls face and devote themselves to changing the circumstances. In this third and final section of the book, we describe pathways for transformation for educational institutions. We draw upon the inspirational work of scholars and activists dedicated to educational reform and transformation. Thus far, we have documented the amazing ways girls have individually and collectively remained resilient and resisted pressures working to suppress and oppress their humanity. We believe that adults can (and should) nurture the safety

DOI: 10.4324/9781003111535-8

of—and encourage rebellion in—girls, while also working to transform the oppressive systems in which girls find themselves.

Youth Activism

Activism that is led by girls and informed by girls' experiences in school is one avenue for the transformation of educational systems. Scholars of youth activism have argued that it is important to explore how girls define activism when seeking to understand their engagement. For example, Taft (2010, 2014) who studied girls' activism globally, asserts that understanding girls' civic engagement and activism might require first redefining and conceptualizing politics and engagement. She found that sometimes girls will say that they are not interested in politics but describe holding critical perspectives on many deeply political issues. In Phase 2 of our project, we asked girls about their ideas about activism, whether they saw themselves as activists, and what role they felt young adults could play in changing problems in society. The girls described activism in ways similar to what we have found in other studies of girls' activism (Brinkman, 2016). They defined activism as caring about an issue and then taking actions to make change happen, making their voices heard, and standing up for what they believe in. Rose (12th grade) described why she believes it is important to engage in activism:

> I think that that's important to make sure your peers know that and the people around you, 'cause I feel like that just makes it [a] more safe and comfortable environment. I also think if you want to change something, if [it] bothers you, like, [ask yourself] what can you do to change it?

Some of the girls talked about participating in activism outside of the school—in the form of attending formal protests or promoting change through social media. Laura (12th grade) shared that "I always try to go to the protests and stuff when I can. I'm on the texting list for Sierra Club and Daily-Action-type things." Rose (12th grade) described having attended multiple marches about various issues she cared about.

We asked the girls we interviewed whether they used social media to promote social change. Social media offers an easily accessible source for engagement in social movements for girls, many of whom combine online and offline modes of activism (Hirzalla and Van Zoonen, 2010). Engaging in activism online can influence offline activism, whether girls use social media to express their opinions about current events or to find information (Valenzuela, 2013). Girls use blogging (Keller, 2015), Twitter (Keller, 2018; Ringrose and Mendes, 2018), and various other forms of media and social media to learn about feminist social issues and engage in activism (Mendes et al., 2019). Mia (11th grade) described using social media for activism: "I talk about a lot of political stuff, like, when I'm on Twitter." Rose (12th grade) described using Facebook to educate others, especially adults in her life, about feminist issues:

> There's a lot of, like—recently, I think there's been an uprise in pages to do with feminism and just making girls feel like empowered and stuff or things about, like ... videos about girls not, like, shaving or videos about what it means to be a girl or slam poetry talking about sexual assault or harassment, stuff like that. I always share those things 'cause I feel like—I don't know. And I always say "This is so important," or, "Watch." Or even things with the election, how women should feel about it or the march they had in [a nearby city], like that stuff. I think that's mostly what I use my Facebook for just 'cause ... since I only have—I mostly have older people [reading my Facebook feed]. It's like, I want them to see that, 'cause ... some parents will show their kids. I think some parents are close-minded still. But if they see stuff ... they kind of understand more what the younger generations are about.

Activism for School Transformation

One avenue for activism includes participating in formal clubs or organizations whose mission is to address social issues. Many of the students we interviewed at Our Lady of Guadalupe Catholic High School were members of the Diversity Club. Students formed this club as an alternative to a Gay-Straight Alliance, which they wanted to form but were not allowed to do so by the school administration. Maria (12th grade) described how it unfolded:

> Well, originally, we wanted to start a GSA, a Gay-Straight Alliance, but that was shut down. And so, they were like, "Well, if you want to do something like that you have to make it very broad," so they were like, "Diversity Club."

The Diversity Club also held service events and organized actions to try to build awareness in the school about societal issues. For example, after Trump was elected, students displayed posters with positive quotes and empowering statements. Joy (12th grade) described the Diversity Club as part service-oriented and part debate:

> It mostly just discusses problems we see at the school and debate because of how current-event-oriented it is, it's a very progressive atmosphere. And there's basically—[laughs] everybody's that in Debate is in Diversity Club, and everybody in Diversity Club is in Debate. So, it's mostly a discussion and sometimes volunteering.

School organizations, like the Diversity Club, can offer safe spaces for students and provide opportunities for individual and group transformation. Rose (12th grade) talked about what she saw as the benefits of having the club and how it created a space in the school for students to feel accepted:

> But I feel it's good that we have a club like that because it gives people the opportunity to feel accepted and to feel comfortable. We want you to have a space that you can trust at school, and if that's the only place that you can have that, be comfortable. Well, I—we need to work on something, obviously, but that's a good start.

Research supports these students' views that clubs can provide important safe havens for students. Feminist clubs/groups in schools can offer spaces for girls to examine their lived experiences regarding social identities, educate themselves and others about social issues, create allyships, and develop strategies for sparking change within schools (Brown, 2016; Cayleff et al., 2011; Kim and Ringrose, 2018).

Although they were allowed to form the Diversity Club, students reported that they were often restricted regarding their activities. Erin (11th grade) shared that the school's administration did not fully support the club, saying:

> I feel like it is supported to an extent. If we were to want to check out of school to go to a march or something, they would be like, "No, you can't do that." Depending on what it was for, it also would be different.

Rose (12th grade) talked about some of the activities the club initiated and how educators in the school responded:

> So, we have a Diversity Club here, and during, like, the Black Lives Matter movement last year, I think we had signs up saying, "We stand in solidarity" and "Black Lives Matter" hashtagged, and we got in trouble. And people were writing white supremacist things on the posters and the principal and the teachers—some teachers were pissed off and they made us take down the posters and said that we couldn't do that. And then, this year with the election—I know the election's kind of different—we weren't doing anything against Trump, but we were doing stuff that was making sure everybody knew that they felt safe and we support everybody. And they wouldn't let us have posters like that cause it was too political or stuff. So, anytime that somebody does try to speak out about it or bring awareness to it even—if it's not trying to solve the issue, just bringing awareness to it—we are told we're not allowed to do it 'cause it's too controversial. So, then you feel you can't really fix it, because every time you try, you get yelled at for it.

Dress Code Protest

The student interviewees also talked about other times they tried to engage in transformative change in the school and how the administration thwarted their efforts. As we described in Chapter 6, Our Lady of Guadalupe Catholic High School changed the dress code to require girls to wear tights under their skorts throughout the school year. The students were informed of this change during an assembly in which they were told numerous disturbing messages that reinforced rape myths, the sexualization of girls, and toxic stereotypes about masculinity. Girls in the school organized a formal protest against the proposed changes to the uniform policy, with approximately 50 students writing letters to the dean about their concerns. The girls articulated their objections to the policy, including that it was unfair to girls, that it sexualized girls, and that it was being enforced in problematic ways that led the girls to feel unsafe.

This protest organized at Our Lady of Guadalupe was similar to protests against sexualizing dress codes which have taken place in schools throughout the United States and around the world. For example, in 2014, students at a suburban school in New Jersey started the campaign #IAMMOREHTHANADISTRACTION after the girls in a math class were forced to stand in front of the room to have their shorts or skirts measured using the "fingertip rule" (Zaslow, 2018). A number of girls in the school were upset by this experience, the school's dress code, and being told that they were responsible for the boys being distracted in school. With their parents' support, the students organized a protest on social media and requested a meeting with the school's principal. The students had three main discussion points for their meeting with the principal, including 1) educators and administrators should focus on teaching boys to respect girls instead of blaming girls when boys feel distracted, 2) they should give parents and students the authority to determine appropriate dress, and 3) they should be working to change society's stereotypical attitudes about women. The students reported that the meeting was successful and the principal and school agreed to review and revise the dress code policy.

Unfortunately, at Our Lady of Guadalupe, the students received less supportive responses to their protest of the dress code. Maria (12th grade) shared that the school did hold a meeting to discuss the dress code change and how girls felt about it, but she left feeling even worse than she had before the meeting:

> We had a meeting after everything that happened—of the student leaders and faculty and the admin to talk about what we could do to fix this. And it was supposed to be this productive town hall meeting. But what ended up happening was some of the faculty were saying, "Well, girls can't wear the knee highs because it looks immodest, and you don't want to look like that. It looks kind of slutty" and they were

referencing to porn. Yeah, it was very … It was just another side moment—I remember just coming back, like, crying to teachers just because it was frustrating to see teachers who were adults maintain this stereotype and this idea. Instead [of] having a productive way to tell us, "No, we're just going to keep it by [the] rules," … they sort of tagged along this other stereotype.

Some students reported that initially they felt the dean of students acknowledged their feelings and was responsive to the protest letters, but none of their requests led to a policy change. The dean later enforced the policy and told the girls that it was not his decision. Rose (12th grade) described how this reflected the culture of the school, that students are not allowed to raise their concerns about some topics and that the administration would not listen to those students who do try to speak out:

> Well, I asked the dean what that was about and why? But there's also this thing at the school where you're not allowed to basically argue or bring attention to certain topics. So, that's kind of an issue because, obviously, nobody wants to get in trouble for saying something. And basically, we can't argue our way out of it 'cause they don't listen anyways, so it's like—I mean, there's, like, a few girls in our school who do say stuff about it, obviously, but it's not a big enough group to be heard, I guess.

Conversations with both girls and educators suggested that the administration often made decisions in a top-down manner, sometimes behind closed doors. One educator described that his perception is that the administration will listen to student concerns but are rarely influenced by their requests:

MR. WALKER: I wasn't sure how it's gone when there's been pushback, but I do think the administration at least gives off the impression, at least to myself and to other sources as well, that they do listen to students. I don't know how much student input has a say with a decision made at the school, but I think the administration absolutely listens to students. I don't think they tell them, "No, we're not gonna listen to your thoughts."

INTERVIEWER: So, your perception is that at least the administration will listen?

MR. WALKER: Yeah, absolutely.

INTERVIEWER: Make the decision they're gonna make, but they'll hear them out.

MR. WALKER: Exactly, that's what I perceive here.

Rules in school often reflect the philosophical and political viewpoints of the adults in power—when students challenge these rules, it might reflect differences in perspectives about worldviews (Raby, 2012). Very few school conduct codes are developed with participation from youth. Even those educators who express they would support the inclusion of youth voices have rarely found ways to genuinely integrate them into the school processes (2012). Is it any surprise, then, that students would challenge rules that are made without their input?

Exposing OLG

During the summer of 2020 (while we were writing this book), we became aware of a Twitter campaign called "Exposing OLG" that was started by alumni at Our Lady of Guadalupe. The initial tweets described the purpose of the campaign, which was organized anonymously:

> As promised: An EXPOSING THREAD on the racism, sexism, and xenophobia committed and/or swept under the rug by the students, teachers, and admin of Our Lady of Guadalupe. I have compiled stories from current and graduated students and will be sharing under this thread. I will first be sharing the stories about teachers and administration failing to support their most marginalized students at OLG. Then, I will be sharing stories of racist students left unaccountable for their racism.

The thread was an opportunity to bring light to issues within the school and was a call for transformation. The campaign was a compelling and well-organized example of using social media for activism. Stories were posted with names redacted to protect the students. The stories included a wide range of concerns, with many of the same stories that we heard during our interviews three years prior.

The campaign author named patterns of disturbing behavior in the school, including specific individual stories, but also made clear that the incidents were not isolated:

> OLG has a pattern of covering up sexual assaults and harassment, leaving no support for the victims. Notoriously, they covered up a sexual assault because the male student had a scholarship to play football and "didn't want his life to be ruined because of one mistake."

There were numerous examples of sexual assaults and the school's response, including the incident we described in Chapter 6 when a student was sexually assaulted during an international trip with the school. Another thread called out the policing of girls' bodies and the dress code change that required girls to wear tights under their skorts. The tweets also described the disturbing way this policy was communicated to the students:

> In one instance, all girls at OLG had to report to the auditorium to be reprimanded for wearing our skirts/skorts "too short." The male students ridiculed us as we were being punished, saying things like, "The girls are getting in trouble for being sluts.

Another thread focused on experiences of racism in the school, enacted by both adults and other students. These stories shared how students of color faced racial slurs, ridicule, had racist "jokes" directed at them in the classroom, and more.

The campaign author pointed out explicitly that the stories shared were indicative of problems within the culture of the school. "If you haven't picked up on it already, there is a toxic culture of racism, sexism, homophobia and xenophobia at OLG." The campaign called for transformation in the school, demanding accountability for the actions of specific teachers and administrators. The thread also included a call for transformation on the part of students at Our Lady of Guadalupe:

> On this thread, I will be sharing stories of racism committed by students and naming them directly. If you see yourself on here, I want you to ask yourself: Have I apologized for this harm? What actions am I taking now to mitigate the harm that I may have caused in the past? If I have changed, have I taken the necessary steps to learn why my behavior was wrong? If you see your friends on here, ask yourself: Why did I let my friends behave in this way? Why was I complacent instead of educating them knowing they'd listen to me? How can I talk to them now that I know what they did was wrong??? While these students are 100% responsible for the things they've said, OLG is equally responsible for allowing it & not educating students about why this is wrong. My goal is not to "cancel" these students but rather to create the conditions for accountability within the OLG community and call on students to actively work on what it means to be anti-racist.

While the Twitter campaign unfolded, a group of alumni sent a petition to the school's administration with 500+ signatures asking that the school address issues of racism and develop a plan to create an inclusive environment in the school. The Twitter campaign and the letter to the administration were both examples of ways girls (and young women) used activism to advocate for transformative change within the school.

Planting Seeds

Unfortunately, in addition to learning about girl-led activism inside schools, we heard about push-back and the lack of support from adults in the schools. The girls we interviewed shared some of the barriers they experienced while engaging in activism, including feeling unsure of their perspective and worrying about how others would react to them. They also said that lack of support from—and being dismissed by—adults were barriers to engaging in activism. Students described limits placed on their attempts to engage in truly transformative efforts within the school. While we were disappointed to hear about the opposition from adults, we were not surprised. Transformative change can be perceived by adults in the school as a threat to their positions of power. As we discussed earlier in the book, the space girls are given to excel as Super Girls affords them some leadership opportunities, as long as their efforts are sanctioned by adults with authority. However, challenging the adults in the school, commenting on the problems with systems of power, or engaging in activities that would change the school dynamics were often suppressed.

When we asked educators about students who engaged in activism or social change, some teachers responded that they saw these actions as immature, inappropriate, or rebellious, rather than legitimate expressions of concerns. For example, Mr. Baker commented:

> The only issue is, like, sometimes when 9th graders do it or try to do it, it's a little ridiculous. And I think the girls here and the guys ... do feel empowered to do stuff like that. But it's not always, you know, like, really well-thought-out. Sometimes, it's just a reaction to something they didn't like about what you did.

Raby (2012) found similar assertions from some educators who conceptualized rule-breaking as intentional power-grabbing and rule-following as demonstrating respect for authority. Some educators we interviewed said that they did not see girls engaged in activism while they were in high school but did know alumni who were active after they graduated. Ms. Powell said:

> I just don't see it that much in high school. I've noticed that with a lot of the students that I've friended since they graduated who have gotten to be somewhat activist. But it's usually when they go to college or graduate that they start to engage. And like I said, I can usually tell who they're going to be, you know, before they do it. They're the ones that will challenge you in class ... and, you know, engage in those debates.

Some educators expressed their support for girls actively working on social change. Dr. Wilson described activist girls in this way:

> Well, I think they can make huge, a huge impact. I'm all about girl power. We have a fair number, a good handful of girls who are either involved in our Peace and Justice Club or girls who are really good natural leaders, and it's helping them channel that into a positive direction.

Mrs. Smith noted the level of engagement in social issues by girls at OLG:

> I think their voices are heard. I think they are vocal, are not afraid to voice their opinion…. And to use social media, you know, to further promote–I'm amazed at the quality of their [community] service and the agencies, and for some of these kids, that it's not just putting in the hours. That they really have this long-term commitment, and relationship, … if not to change, at least in nurturing and caring. But I think they're thinking more globally.

Adults in a school can play a crucial role in supporting girl-led activism. "Where we find feminism matters; from whom we find feminism matters" (Ahmed, 2016, p. 5). We asked the girls we interviewed how adults can serve as better allies for girls in their activism work. The girls shared that they wanted adults to listen to them, to start conversations and offer education about social issues, to lead by example, to offer girls opportunities to lead projects and try new activities, and to provide support and scaffolding for the girls in their education and activism.

In the report of the National Women's Law Center (2019), "Dress Coded II," activism around the problematic aspects of dress codes found in the first report (2018) came from students, parents, teachers, and school staff. Importantly, regardless of the source of activism, centering girls' experiences of being dress-coded was at the heart of the work. In other words, one recommendation from the follow-up report is the necessity for dress codes to be co-created with students. The report describes activism from women and girls within schools which encouraged administrators to create dress code committees and inspired conversations about enforcement of policies.

In a thoughtful exploration of the challenges for intergenerational allies in scaffolding girl-led-activism, Edell, Brown, and Tolman (2013) describe the necessity of allowing for space and deep listening by adults. This could involve critiques, questions, and criticism that challenges adult-held notions of activism, feminism, and politics. In their reflections on their work with Sexualization Protest: Action Resistance Knowledge (SPARK), they write, "We live with the starts, stops and contradictions, listen deeply to girls' voices and experiences, learn from insights, successes and mistakes, and ultimately trust and work with girls' power" (p. 281). It is by holding space for contradictions and complications that we as adults can learn the best ways to be supportive of girls and challenge existing systems of discrimination, harassment, and oppression.

Looking internationally at girls' activism, Moletsane (2018) documented how adult researchers supported girls' activism—specifically activism in the form of a girl-led march against sexual violence in South Africa. Adult allies were careful to note and take precautions against the potential risk for violence or retaliation against the march (having local authorities march along with the group) and use their relative power and privilege to get the necessary permits for the march. Beyond that, the adults made space to listen to the girls and young women as they developed advertising, signs and messaging, invitations, and a program for community members to gather after the march. "In this and similar communities, it is this intergenerational collaboration that is likely to inform effective and sustainable policy and programming at various levels" (p. 249).

Despite the many challenges girls faced, they engaged in activism inside and outside Our Lady of Guadalupe Catholic High School. They named when events happening in their school were harming them (from sexualization to racism), and they came together to support each other and fight for change. They did not always achieve the outcomes they were looking for, but their energy was not wasted. The Twitter campaign that the alumni organized demonstrated that even though the girls were not able to change the school while they were students, they did not give up. The process of activism is transformative—not only for the systems but also for the girls engaging in it. Activism plants seeds that might take time to grow.

References

Ahmed, S. (2016). *Living a feminist life*. Duke University Press.

Brinkman, B.G. (2016). Promoting adolescent girls' civic engagement and activism. In A.L. Bos and M.C. Schneider (Eds)., *The Political Psychology of Women in U.S. Politics*. 34–50. Routledge/Taylor & Francis Group.

Brown, L.M. (2016). *Powered by girl: A field guide for supporting youth activists*. Beacon Press.

Cayleff, S., Herron, M., Cormier, C., Wheeler, S., Chávez-Arteaga, A., Spain, J., and Dominguez, C. (2011). Oral history and "girls' voices": The young women's studies club as a site of empowerment. *Journal of International Women's Studies*, 12 (4), 22–44. https://vc.bridgew.edu/jiws/vol12/iss4/2.

Edell, D., Brown, L.M., and Tolman, D. (2013). Embodying sexualisation: When theory meets practice in intergenerational feminist activism. *Feminist Theory*, 14 (3), 275–284. https://doi.org/10.1177/1464700113499844.

Hirzalla, F. and van Zoonen, L. (2010). Beyond the online/offline divide: How youth's online and offline civic activities converge. *Social Science Computer Review* 29(4), 481–498. https://doi.org/10.1177/0894439310385538.

Keller, J. (2015) *Girls' feminist blogging in a postfeminist age*. Routledge.

Keller, J. (2018). Crop tops and solidarity selfies: The disruptive politics of girls' hashtag politics. *Mediated Girlhoods: New Explorations of Girls' Media Culture*, 2, 157–173.

Kim, C. and Ringrose, J. (2018). "Stumbling upon feminism": Teenage girls' forays into digital and school-based feminisms. *Girlhood Studies*, 11(2), 46–62. www.doi.org/10.3167/ghs.2018.110205.

Mendes, K., Keller, J., and Ringrose, J. (2019). Digitized narratives of sexual violence: Making sexual violence felt and known through digital disclosures. *New Media & Society*, 21(6), 1290–1310.

Moletsane, R. (2018). "Stop the war on women's bodies": Facilitating a girl-led march against sexual violence in a rural community in South Africa. *Studies in Social Justice*, 12(2), 235–250. doi:10.26522/ssj.v12i2.1655.
National Women's Law Center. (2018). *Dress Coded.* Black girls, bodies and bias in D.C. schools. https://nwlc-ciw49tixgw5lbab.stackpathdns.com/wp-content/uploads/2018/04/Final_nwlc_DressCodeReport.pdf.
National Women's Law Center. (2019). *Dress Coded* II. Protests, progress, and power in D.C. schools. https://nwlc.org/resources/dresscoded-ii.
Raby, R. (2012). *School rules: Obedience, discipline, and elusive democracy.* University of Toronto Press.
Ringrose, J. and Mendes, K. (2018). Mediated affect and feminist solidarity: Teens' using Twitter to challenge "rape culture" in and around school. In T. Sampson, D. Ellis, and S. Maddison (Eds) *Affect and Social Media*. Rowman & Littlefield.
Taft, J.K. (2010). *Rebel girls: Youth activism and social change across the Americas.* New York University Press.
Taft, J.K. (2014). The political lives of girls. *Sociology Compass*, 8(3), 259–267. doi:10.1111/soc4.12135.
Valenzuela, S. (2013). Unpacking the use of social media for protest behavior: The role of information, opinion expression, and activism. *American Behavioral Scientist*, 57 (7), 920–942. doi:10.1177/0002764213479375.
Zaslow, E. (2018). #Iammorethanadistraction: Connecting local body polities to a digital feminist movement. In J. Keller and M. E. Ryan (Eds), *Emergent Feminisms* (pp. 93–107). Routledge. www.taylorfrancis.com/chapters/edit/10.4324/9781351175463-6/iammorethanadistraction-emilie-zaslow.

Chapter 8

Radical Healing and Community Transformation

Start Anywhere, Follow It Everywhere

INTERVIEWER: *If you could change anything about girls' experiences in your school, what would it be?*

MR. WALKER: *The magic wand is for the girls here to understand that equality matters. And, actually not for the girls, [but] for the boys to realize that.*

One aspect of transformation involves shifting our goals away from encouraging girls to be "resilient" in the face of oppressive systems toward creating conditions in which girls can thrive. In this chapter, we draw upon the concept of radical healing, which transcends coping with stressors and learning to survive oppression, to focus on the experience of thriving (French et al., 2020, p. 19). We also examine how educators navigate their own identities, oppressions, privileges, power, and powerlessness as well as their healing journeys. In order to create safe spaces where girls can thrive, educators need resources, appropriate policies and training, and supportive administrators. We situate our work among scholars who assert that recovery and healing are necessary for people experiencing oppression to work toward liberation and transformation (Brown, 2017). We advocate for processes that promote reciprocal transformation, including intergenerational work that fosters healing for adults, changes systems, and creates safe spaces for girls. While we work to transform schools, we recognize the need to address the negative impact of current systems on girls and educators and develop avenues for healing.

Healing for Educators

While educators play an essential role in supporting girls within schools, they also face challenges and barriers to doing so. Educators need support to be able to engage in their own transformative work. We encourage educators to engage in critical reflection to examine their own pathways to transformation and to ask themselves, "What do we need to heal in ourselves in order to offer a future of any real peace?" (Brown, 2017, p. 164)

DOI: 10.4324/9781003111535-9

Bettina Love (2019) describes the importance of intergenerational healing to transform education. She advocates an abolitionist approach to teaching and emphasizes that the goal for educational spaces should not be merely the survival of marginalized children but creating the conditions in which all children can flourish. She describes that an essential element of this work is for educators to choose wellness in their own lives and to engage in the hard work of building and maintaining that wellness. We believe that a crucial aspect of transforming educational systems includes supporting teachers in their own healing. Educators need to heal the wounds they experienced leading up their time as an educator—including their own experiences of oppressive school systems and the way they navigated discrimination on their paths to become educators. They also need healing from the wounds they acquire as educators.

We believe that many educators enter the profession with the best intentions to support youth and facilitate their growth and development. Despite these good intentions, educators often re-enact the same traumas that they experienced in educational settings. In one study examining how schools integrate restorative justice and practices, an administrator shared that they realized they had engaged in a lot of the same behaviors that they punished students for, adding that "perhaps that is why I am so hard on them" (Winn, 2018). We must recognize the humanity of our educators, including the way their own educational journeys have included narratives of resilience and resistance. Teachers bring into their work their histories of school experiences, both good and bad, which can inform the way they engage with students.

Teachers who have had their own traumatic experiences within school systems related to social identities—experiences of sexism, racism, homophobia, classism, etc.—need healing to engage in transformative work to support students. For example, Ms. Powell shared some of her own experiences fighting for her place in traditionally masculine arenas and disciplines. She talked about how she navigated others' expectations of her as a woman and the pathway she took to be successful. We heard in her narratives her own resilience within oppressive systems as well as her doubts about transformation:

> Maybe it is a patriarchy. Maybe it is out there. I've never really noticed. I will say this: I've learned to work with it. And at this point, I don't know if I'd like it if we ended it too much because I finally feel like I've learned the rules of the game. I don't want to learn a whole new set—and it's not always all bad. The good thing is—let them underestimate you. Let them. That's great. Easier for you to shine, you know, whatever. So, I don't know, just some things like that. My idea of feminism is totally different from what's being promoted on campuses today. Totally opposite. I think we started in the same place, but it's very divergent paths.

Ms. Powell's articulated throughout her interview a desire for girls (and all students) to be successful, as well as skepticism about the possibility for system transformation. Instead of working toward transformation or fighting against the systems as they exist, she advocated for strategic navigations of the rules as they are. At times, she expressed frustration regarding students who resist and articulated that they have unrealistic expectations about the world. We heard in Ms. Powell's narratives that she wants what is best for her students and believes she is helping prepare them for the world we live in—as she experiences it. We wonder how Ms. Powell would approach ideas for system transformation—and the girls who desire it—were she given opportunities for healing of her own experiences of sexism.

Educators need opportunities to heal from the wounds inflicted on them during their careers and within their school environments. Some teachers join the profession because they want to make the world a better place. They see social justice as a key part of their role and think about how to have the greatest impact within the parameters of their jobs. Educational researchers refer to these types of teachers as "idealists" who tend to have high motivation for their work (Marsh, 2015). School environments that suppress transformative work and social justice efforts might more negatively influence these teachers. Individuals who joined the profession to improve social conditions might experience burnout if they find themselves in school systems where sexism and racism appear rampant and where there is a lack of commitment from administrators to acknowledge or address these problems.

Veteran teachers are also faced with the daunting challenge of maintaining a long-term commitment to activism both inside and outside of schools. Mrs. Smith talked about her commitment to feminism throughout her life and how that manifested in choices she made within her marriage, as a mother, and as a teacher. She also shared ways she had experienced some activism fatigue over the years and had at times become more passive. She shared, "I was such a fighter then and educated my husband. I thought we'd reached this point and I realize now that I've lost the fight thinking that the battle's won." She went on to describe her realization that the fight for gender equality in schools or in the wider society is far from over. "When you look at women's reproductive rights—that these are white men that are deciding for us.... I thought we had solved this question, and I thought we were so beyond this, and yet, here we go." She talked about how it felt to watch Hillary Clinton run for President and how she was treated and her frustration that there has yet to be a woman president in the United States. She also described that she thought there had been more progress made within schools regarding gender equality but noted that there continued to be issues, particularly related to leadership:

> I think my biggest concern is the student body elections this year when there were, I think, 11 or 12 candidates and only one female. And it was

> the first time that I'm like, something's wrong with this picture. It's fascinating in my class when we go to group work that I do see that the girls will defer to the boys. I really thought that was changing, but I don't know. This election, with the student body, has helped me see something. And is this a pattern or not? I don't know.

Mrs. Smith described her recent reawakening to the issues of gender inequality throughout society. She shared her concern that young women are not aware of all of the choices that could be available to them because so much of society has convinced them that we have achieved equality: "I think they [young women] think that they're equal. And then we've had this backslide. I mean, it's hard to put your finger on it, you know, and I'm just kind of opening my eyes again." As a token of appreciation for participating in the interviews, we gave each educator a copy of Lyn Mikel Brown's book *Powered by Girl: A Field Guide for Supporting Youth Activists*, which has been a source of inspiration for us. We invited educators to follow up and stay in conversation with us—to reach out if they had other ideas to share or wanted resources as they thought about how they could continue to support the girls in their schools.

Our interview allowed Mrs. Smith to reflect on her lifelong commitment to feminism and equality in education—as well as to make connections about events unfolding in her school. Mrs. Smith closed her interview by sharing how much it had influenced her:

> Keep doing your work. Keep doing what you're doing now, but it's opened my heart and mind that we need to find ways to make this part of our thinking, planning. It makes me more aware. I think it's time to refine and bring it back out. So, I'm working at it. Thank you.

While we do not claim that one interview about girls' experiences in schools can heal educators' wounds, we do believe that these conversations are essential and can spark reflection and renewed commitment. In schools where teachers are consistently told to stop asking questions, to trust the administration, and to focus on their classroom teaching, the opportunities for these discussions become harder to find. We hoped that our study was the start of the conversation, not the end.

We feel so much gratitude to Mrs. Smith, all the educators who participated in our study, and all educator activists who are working towards transformation within their own schools. We see you. We hear your stories. We support you on your journey of healing and transformation.

Transformative Policies, Pedagogies, and Practices

We believe that it is possible to transform our educational institutions and practices to create environments that sustain the wellness of educators and allow all children to thrive. We know that girls and educators are hungry for that transformation. In our interviews, we asked educators and girls about changes they wanted to see—in schools and in the world. We describe the ideas and suggestions from girls and educators below as we detail various policies, pedagogies and practices designed to transform educational spaces.

There is no one-size-fits-all approach to transformation—each school system must determine the pathway that is best for them. We draw on the principles of Frieze and Wheatley (2011) who documented communities around the world that embraced transformational change to address local problems. They recommend that communities learn from each other about what has worked for them and suggest that it is better to scale across rather than scale up. Instead of using a top-down strategy where communities attempt to replicate interventions that others have used, they argue that transformational change happens horizontally. Each community must experiment to find what is right for them. We suggest that schools take this same approach.

We offer strategies (many of which are evidence-based) that have worked in other school communities as ideas and suggestions to inform and inspire. Each school should explore these strategies and adapt them to that school's unique situation. Below we describe a range of approaches, practices, and policies that can aid in the process of transformation. We offer brief explanations and examples and encourage educators to dig deeper into the ideas that inspire them. We provide a variety of ideas, as there are many entry points into educational transformation. Choose one that is meaningful to you—as change begins to happen, you can decide where to grow and expand. Too often, we become paralyzed when facing large systemic problems. If we do not see a clear solution that will fix everything, we hesitate to do anything. Frieze and Wheatley (2011) offer us this wisdom from communities who have embraced transformation: start anywhere; follow it everywhere.

Building Coalitions

Transformative work can be challenging and time-consuming—but no one has to (or can!) do it alone. Building coalitions with others who share your values can help you embark on the journey of transformation. Coalitions create spaces for support, new ideas, personal and organizational growth, and developing deep, long-lasting relationships that help to sustain the work. For example, Teacher Activist Groups (TAGs) can provide one source of support for teachers who are invested in transformative work. TAGs include teachers and their allies who "meet to engage in joint inquiry into questions of pedagogy and policy, knowledge and resource sharing through conferences and curriculum fairs, and organizing to advocate for their students and schools" (Niesz, 2018). A nationwide coalition called the National Network of Teacher Activist Groups connects TAGs across the United States. TAGs are generally composed of teachers and other school personnel and tend to be intergenerational and represent a diversity of demographic identities. Specific TAGs have unique histories and local emphases, but they do have some shared goals, including a desire for the development of school practices that promote equity and justice and value diversity. They call for curriculum and pedagogy that will empower and liberate youth and engage them in critical dialogues about diversity. TAGs engage in consciousness-raising and education about issues happening within schools and share knowledge with other teacher organizations about best practices. They also frequently engage in advocacy including protests, letter-writing campaigns, rallies, and speaking at public meetings with the goal of influencing school administrators, school boards, and even state and federal legislators.

Community groups can also support the transformation of schools and school systems. Educational advocacy groups outside the school system can leverage their outsider status to raise concerns without fear of retaliation or the threat of job loss. These groups can also develop alliances and coalitions of stakeholders from many groups including teachers, parents, students, mental health professionals, researchers, youth-serving organizations, and others. For example, Britney Brinkman is a founding member of the Black Girls Equity Alliance in Pittsburgh, Pennsylvania. The Black Girls Equity Alliance (BGEA) is composed of individuals, community-based organizations, universities, and government entities that collaborate with Black girls and acknowledge that their lives and experiences are unique within existing societal constructs (Brinkman et al., 2019). There are currently over 30 partner organizations. BGEA's mission is accomplished by informing providers, communities, and systems about best practices for supporting Black girls and advocating for policy changes that will improve their lives. BGEA has worked consistently on educational reform in Western Pennsylvania, addressing issues in schools including sexual harassment, the need for improved sexual education, revising dress codes and discipline codes, removing police from schools, culturally responsive mental health in schools, and more.

Transformative Pedagogies

Feminist pedagogy, liberation pedagogy, and abolitionist teaching offer models for creating transformative educational spaces. Our work has been informed by pedagogical writings emphasizing the role of education in promoting justice, such as Freire's (1970) *Pedagogy of the Oppressed* and hooks' (1994) *Teaching to Transgress: Education as the Practice of Freedom*. Pedagogy centered on collaborative learning and social justice initiatives promote the conditions necessary for learning to occur. The girls we interviewed want intersectional pedagogies centered on social justice. They recognize that systems of power and social identities influence each other. When asked about what changes she would like to see, Mia (11th grade) responded:

> I think that's the magic question that [laughs] nobody knows—is that it's, like, what causes what? Because it's clear that everything is intertwined. Like racism, sexism, bigotry, like, all of those things ... exist in the same circle, but it's hard to figure out what created what. So, like, what's the thing that you go for first? And I think, like, I would probably say ... I don't know how to fix it [laughs], so I don't know what direction I would go first. But I would probably say, like, education and empathy.

Feminist pedagogy can empower individual students and offer a method of systemic change, challenging the way schools are designed to recreate inequalities and norms of society. Integrating feminist pedagogies into schools can help create pathways for creating gender equality in schools. Tina (12th grade) described her desire for equal treatment:

> It would definitely be equality between boys and girls. Just overall. I just want to walk in somewhere and be treated the same as—like, I don't want to be talked badly about because I'm a girl or because I'm on the drill team or because I'm whatever. It doesn't matter.

Educators can utilize feminist pedagogies in K-12 schools in numerous ways. For example, Martin (et al.) (2017) describes her work integrating feminist pedagogy into an alternative school. She was concerned about the degree of sexism and sexual harassment that girls in the school experienced and recognized the impact these experiences had on the mental health of the students. Her goal was to offer a pathway for transformation by creating a "classroom space where the girls in the school could experience 'what could be': a classroom of their own creation" (p. 6). Ileana Jiménez has worked for decades in feminist and social justice education. She has modeled ways to bring intersectional feminist teaching into K-12 education. She launched her blog, *Feminist Teacher* in 2009 to share her experiences with other educators.

Liberatory pedagogies have been integrated into classrooms and entire school systems. For example, the Mississippi Freedom Schools began in 1963 when a field secretary of the Student Nonviolent Coordinating Committee wrote a proposal to create Freedom Schools in Mississippi to revitalize the civil rights movement (Ayers, 2016). Freedom schools offered an alternative to models of education that focus on control and obedience. The liberation model provided in freedom schools taught students that they are free and full human beings. Thus, they are "inherently (and not contingently) valuable, both they and the world they inherit are works in progress and still under construction, that as humans they are paradoxically completely unique and simultaneously the same as all others" (Ayers, 2016, p. 158). Schools based in liberation pedagogies focus on producing fully developed humans who believe in their own innate value and who work to transform their own lives. Such a liberation model would support Erin's (11th grade) desire to decrease judgment of other people and be able to see each other's shared humanity:

> I feel people need to stop worrying about everyone else and just focus on things that they can do to better themselves, and by bettering yourself, you can better everyone else who also can better themselves. So, if people would stop judging women for being smart, and stop judging women for speaking their mind, and stuff like that, I think we would just realize how we're all so similar. We're all so much more alike than we think.

Bettina Love (2019) describes her vision for abolitionist pedagogies to transform school environments and provide students the opportunity to thrive. Abolitionist teaching recognizes and honors the humanity of children in school. Love advocates for schools that are free from police, metal detectors, high-stakes testing, and suspensions. Abolitionist pedagogies teach children about racism, homophobia, sexism, and other forms of discrimination and privilege. They also provide students with loving and joyful educational experiences and recognize the need to address trauma in students' lives and promote wellness and mental health. This approach to education can foster inclusive educational environments and build community. Maria (12th grade) described her wish that her school would be more welcoming for Latinx students:

> I guess I would adjust—make the community about all aspects because we pride ourselves on being a really big community and I love that, and I love having people to go to. But I just wish that was for other people as well ... because for me, maybe I have that just because I've been a leader. But someone, let's say ... my friend who is a Latina and is more on the outskirts ... maybe [things can change so] she can feel that community too.

Transforming Policies

Unfortunately, educational policies can often become barriers to transformation in schools. As we described in Chapter 6, dress code policies in schools are often permeated with sexist and racist language and frequently implemented in disproportionate ways, policing girls and Black, indigenous, people of color students. These policies contribute to an atmosphere that promotes sexual violence and perpetuates harmful stereotypes about masculinity. State and federal laws can also have chilling effects on attempts to transform schools into spaces where all students can thrive. The No Child Left Behind Act pressured schools to change their curriculum to focus more on improving test scores (Walker, 2014). Teachers reported avoiding discussions of diversity and current political events—such as the election of President Obama in 2008—because they worried it would detract from time spent teaching material students needed to know for the annual tests (Journell, 2010). Recent attempts to ban critical race theory in schools have affected educators' ability to talk about a range of topics related to diversity, equity, and inclusion.

One body of educational policies which have had particularly detrimental effects on school environments include zero tolerance or no tolerance policies. No tolerance policies have become popular in schools in the United States and are often utilized as attempts to address concerns about bullying (Brinkman, 2016). Numerous scholars have found that these policies are ineffective at addressing bullying and often result in marginalized children being punished when they defend themselves against bullying and harassment (Brown, Chesney-Lind, and Stein, 2007; Crenshaw et al., 2015; Klein, 2012; Stein, 2001). These policies are contributing to the school-to-prison pipeline and pushout of girls of color because the policies are disproportionately applied and result in punishment of BIPOC students (Crenshaw et al., 2015; Morris, 2016). These policies have created school environments that emphasize discipline and often criminalize normal adolescent behaviors. In many schools, it has become commonplace for police officers to intervene in situations that are far from criminal.

Monique Morris (2016) offers insights into school-based strategies that can provide educational justice for marginalized students today—especially Black girls and other girls of color. Morris has documented in her work the myriad ways that Black girls are pushed out of school systems, often because authorities criminalize their expressions of dissent to injustice in schools. Morris provides suggestions for how schools can become sites for educational justice including the need for policy reform, suspending exclusionary discipline, removing police from schools, and utilizing restorative solutions.

In many schools, one important aspect of transformation will require changing or abolishing policies that reinforce the status quo and create harmful environments. Policy reviews are needed at the school and district levels, as well as advocacy at state and federal levels. We do not suggest that every school adopt cookie-cutter policies; rather, we recommend that a review of existing policies and development of new ones should utilize some key guiding principles:

- Involve a group of stakeholders in the review and development process. The group should include students, family members, community members, teachers, support staff, and administrators.
- Gather data about the implementation of policies to examine whether they are being disproportionately applied to specific groups of students based on gender, race, sexual orientation, and/ or other aspects of identity.
- Ensure that policies are inclusive and explicitly address the impact of discrimination on children's experiences.

- Provide training and support for educators to appropriately implement new policies.
- Engage in ongoing assessment and revision of policies.

One area that we specifically recommend that schools conduct policy change is regarding dress codes. As we have described throughout the book, dress code policies that sexualize girls' bodies are harmful to them and teach all students toxic messages about gender. Several of our participants noted that they desire a change in how schools police girls' bodies and choices through dress codes. Mrs. Moore said, "I wish that the school would just let them be in terms of how they look and present themselves.... And take away that focus. I think that not focusing on it would benefit the girls." Ms. Jones, a middle school educator, also talked about wanting schools to shift their focus away from regulating girls' attire:

> I mentioned that the dress code on a free dress day is more likely to be strict for the girls than the boys. And that if pressed—and I'm like, well, why, why is that? Why can't they wear, you know, skintight jeans, if that's what everybody wears or whatever it is? ... The response is a little bit problematic in my mind that I've heard. I have heard in the past, "Well, we don't want, you know, the boys seeing the, you know, getting ideas." You know, you don't want them to, or, I don't know, just sort of like, "Whoa, nice young ladies don't dress that way." ... And I think it's more an education piece on, on the faculty side. I don't think that they're aware of why that would be problematic or what message is that sending to girls. And also, even if they did, you know, what's the alternate language that we want to use? What can we say? ... Yeah, and there's some, you know—we do have one male faculty member—I think for a lot of things, he just is uncomfortable. He doesn't feel like he has the tools to talk to girls about a lot of things.

Transformative Programs and Practices

Schools can adopt various practices and programs that will support and sustain transformative work. Some programs are designed to specifically promote gender equity in schools and may train educators, students, or both. For example, the REFLECT program was developed to increase teachers' competencies for supporting students without being restricted by gender stereotypes (Kollmayer et al., 2020). The program aims to expand teachers' objective action repertoire (knowledge, teaching methods) as well as their subjective action space (self-efficacy beliefs, implicit theories). Pilot research indicated the program was effective at increasing teachers' actions for promoting gender equality as well as increasing students' awareness of fairness in the classroom and their knowledge of gender differences.

Gender transformative programs (which we describe in Chapter 4) can be utilized in schools to teach critical thinking skills to support youth of all genders in recognizing the detrimental impacts of rigid gender roles (Barker et al., 2007; Miller, 2018). These programs teach children and adolescents to identify and challenge stereotypical messages they receive about gender roles from media, school environments, parents, other adults, peers, and other people and places in society. Several educators spoke to a desire to have more of these types of programs in their schools. Mrs. Greene, a middle school teacher, said, "I think I would really like to find a way to move them [girls] away from the influences of the media." Mrs. Smith, a high school teacher, also discussed the need for more media literacy and other skills for girls:

> I really wish we gave them better skills for critical thinking and deconstructing the media and the message—and the hidden messages—to get them to identify with ... this quest for beauty and the contradictory messages that we see. That we are supposed to be thin, but there's still always the picture of the dessert. But again, I think we've become complacent, and I think we need to re-educate so that they can recognize and make a more conscious choice that "I know what you're selling and I'm not buying." Give them strength. But I think the women's march proved that we can rally quickly or strong.

Gender transformative programming addresses the impact of gender role stereotypes on all people, not just youth who identify as female. Such programming has been used with boys around the world to deconstruct harmful stereotypes about masculinity and for violence prevention programming. When asked about what she would change, Ava (12th grade) described the need for more transformative work regarding masculinity:

> We did a unit in Dr. Brinkman's class about gender and stuff. And I find that men, even though they won't admit it, are definitely put down if they are not masculine enough. Or men don't cry or all of that. I think that I would want to take that away. Or, like, even my boyfriend, he's, "I'm a man and I can't do that." I think that I would want to take that away because I couldn't imagine trying to have to hold that up. Girls have their things too, like wearing a dress. But I don't think anything is holding a girl back from feeling her emotions.

Restorative justice practices can also be provide a path for educational transformation. Some schools have also begun to adopt these practices to foster communities in schools and develop strategies for dealing with conflict. Winn (2018) argues that restorative justice circles can create spaces for participatory democracy within a classroom and for developing equal voices for all community members. Research examining restorative justice has shown that a whole-school approach is the most effective at creating change (González et al., 2019). This approach places the theory and practice directly into academic curriculum and democratizes the practice by integrating students as leaders in restorative justice circles.

Restorative justice practices have the potential to be transformational when implemented as a whole-school approach because they require a paradigm shift about power and purpose in schools. The transition is a move away from compliance and punitive discipline—foci which, as we discussed above, have become endemic in schools in response to no tolerance policies. Restorative practices shift toward a focus on learning, engaging, curiosity, and reparation of harm. This approach also requires a change in the paradigm where adults in the school hold power over students—and administrators hold power over teachers—to a community where all members are seen as fully human, equal participants, and worthy of affirming learning practices. Winn (2018) suggests that transformative justice circles are not only helpful for students but can be used with educators to help them explore their own experiences of education. When educators engage in these practices they can heal from their own harmful experience of education and consider how they can change the way they engage with their students.

Whatever programs or practices schools adopt, it is essential that educators are provided with the necessary support and resources to implement them. When schools or districts frequently introduce new programs or suggest that teachers adopt the latest educational fad, these teachers and administrators will likely experience fatigue and doubt. Educators might become resistant to attempts at transformation if they learn that the efforts will not be sustained and supported. To be successful, schools should adopt programs or practices that align with the values of the administrators, the teachers, and the students and their families. Decision-makers must then demonstrate their commitment to these programs by providing long-term commitment and ongoing support to sustain them.

Supporting Mental Health in Schools

As we have documented in this book, too often schools are places that create trauma for girls. Girls' experiences of sexual harassment and sexual violence in school (as well as outside of school) are pervasive and harm girls' mental health and well-being. When asked what she would change about schools, Dr. Wilson expressed her desire for schools to better address these traumatic experiences:

> My main concern is sexual violence and dating violence. Not the principal now, but when we had [the former principal] here, he just really pulled away from having rape recovery center [staff] ... anybody like that come in and talk to our student body. Now we have teachers who

> are talking a lot more openly about reproductive health. But we're looking at how we do that across the board. I just think there's a lot more of that that goes on and not just the sexual violence.

Educational systems can foster wellness and mental health in schools. Unfortunately, too many school systems in the United States have invested their time, energy, and money into punitive policies and practices. According to a recent report by the ACLU, some 14 million students are in American schools with police but not a single counselor, nurse, psychologist, or social worker. A full 1.7 million students across the United States are attending schools with police officers but no counselors, 6 million students have police but no school psychologists, and 10 million students have police but no social workers. Many schools that do have mental health professionals are often not meeting the recommendations of having at least one counselor and one social worker for every 250 students. An astounding 90% of students in public schools are in schools that do not meet these minimum standards.

In addition to hiring more mental health professionals, school systems need to provide trauma-informed training for educators and culturally responsive mental health resources for students. Trauma-informed approaches in schools recognize that students experience a range of traumas in their homes and communities that can affect how they behave in school. Educators learn to approach students with empathy and compassion and to understand that behaviors that might appear disrespectful or disruptive are, in fact, responses to trauma. For example, students who have experienced trauma might have difficulty sleeping, and, as a result, might fall asleep in class. Students dealing with depression and anxiety might feel irritable and argue with teachers or other adults. Trauma-informed training can help educators make a paradigm shift in understanding these behaviors so that they can respond in a supportive—rather than a punitive—manner. Eve (12th grade) shared her experiences with educators in the school who supported her with mental health:

> I had a Spanish teacher who wasn't really supposed to be a Spanish teacher. That's how I got to know him. Anyways, and he is a much older man like—big, old—like, kind of the stereotypical, wears suit[s] every day, necktie, briefcase kind of thing. Very kind of [an] old-fashioned-type man. And he was the sweetest person I've ever met. He definitely understood. It was definitely at a time when I was going through a lot of really bad depression and anxiety and other stuff. And so he definitely didn't favor me, but he took that into consideration and was like, "Let me help you if I can." And that was awesome.

Culturally responsive mental health training also offers educators skills to recognize signs and symptoms that a student might be struggling with an emotional issue or mental health challenge. Educators also learn ways to respond to students who are in distress and how to connect students with additional services. To give students the best support, educators must learn various ways in which cultural groups understand health and wellness. Also crucial is that educators learn about risk and protective factors for children from marginalized groups. We encourage all schools to provide opportunities to promote strengths and positive mental health in all children, and not wait until a child is struggling.

Moving Beyond Structure

Educational transformation is possible, and we believe it is worth the work involved. In this chapter, we have offered ideas about possible strategies—programs, practices, pedagogies—for transformative work in schools. We hope these will provide tangible support for educators (and anyone else) engaged in this work. For too long we have been working within restrictive, hierarchical, oppressive educational structures and attempting to make tweaks along the way. We are not arguing that any one of these strategies is ideal. In fact, we argue that to truly transform educational institutions, we need a paradigm shift. We need to develop new educational practices—and ways of being—that are rooted in our values. We can then develop and adapt educational structures in an ongoing manner.

References

Ayers, B. (2016). *Demand the impossible!: A radical manifesto*. Haymarket Books.

Barker, G., Ricardo, C., Nascimento, M., and World Health Organization. (2007). *Engaging men and boys in changing gender-based inequity in health: Evidence from programme interventions*.

Brinkman, B.G. (2016). *Detection and prevention of identity-based bullying: Social justice perspectives*. Routledge.

Brinkman, B.G., Goodkind, S., Elliott, K., Joseph, A., and Doswell, W.M. (2019). *Advocating for equity for Black girls: The formation of the Black Girls Equity Alliance*. Gwendolyn J. Elliott Institute.

Brown, A.M. (2017). *Emergent strategy: Shaping change, changing worlds*. AK Press.

Brown, L.M., Chesney-Lind, M., and Stein, N. (2007). Patriarchy matters: Toward a gendered theory of teen violence and victimization. *Violence Against Women*, 13(12), 1249–1273. doi:10.1177/1077801207310430.

Crenshaw, K.W., Ocen, P., and Nanda, J. (2015). *Black girls matter: Pushed out, overpoliced and underprotected*. African American Policy Forum. www.aapf.org/blackgirlsmatter.

Freire, P. (1970). *Pedagogy of the oppressed*. Continuum.

French, B.H. et al. (2020). Toward a psychological framework of radical healing in communities of color. *The Counseling Psychologist*, 48(1), 14–46. doi:10.1177%2F0011000019843506.

Frieze, D. and Wheatley, M. (2011). *Walk out, walk on*. Berrett-Koehler Publishers.

González, T., Sattler, H., and Buth, A.J. (2019). New directions in whole-school restorative justice implementation. *Conflict Resolution Quarterly*, 36(3), 207–220. doi:10.1002/crq.21236.

hooks, b. (1994). *Teaching to transgress: Education as the practice of freedom.*

Journell, W. (2010). The influence of high-stakes testing on high school teachers' willingness to incorporate current political events into the curriculum. *The High School Journal*, 93(3), 111–125. doi:10.1353/hsj.0.0048.

Klein, J. (2012). *The bully society: School shootings and the crisis of bullying in America's schools.* New York University Press.

Kollmayer, M., Schultes, M.T., Lüftenegger, M., Finsterwald, M., Spiel, C., and Schober, B. (2020). REFLECT–A teacher training program to promote gender equality in schools. In *Frontiers in Education*, 5(136), 1–8. Frontiers.

Love, B.L. (2019). *We want to do more than survive: Abolitionist teaching and the pursuit of educational freedom.* Beacon Press.

Marsh, S. (2015, October 25). What type of teacher are you? *The Guardian*. www.theguardian.com/teacher-network/2015/oct/25/what-type-of-teacher-are-you.

Martin, J.L., Nickels, A.E., and Sharp-Grier, M. (Eds). (2017). *Feminist pedagogy, practice, and activism: Improving lives for girls and women.* Taylor & Francis. doi:10.4324/9781315649078.

Miller, E. (2018). Reclaiming gender and power in sexual violence prevention in adolescence. *Violence Against Women*, 24(15), 1785–1793.

Morris, M. (2016). *Pushout: The criminalization of Black girls in schools.* The New Press.

Niesz, T. (2018). Teacher activist groups: What are their missions? How influential are they? *Phi Delta Kappan*, 99(8), 25–29. doi:10.1177/0031721718775674.

Stein, N. (2001). Sexual harassment meets zero-tolerance: Life in K-12 schools. In W. Ayers, B. Dohrn, and R. Ayers (Eds), *Zero tolerance: Resisting the drive for punishment: A handbook for parents, students, educators, and citizens* (pp. 143–154). New Press.

Walker, T. (2014, September 2). The testing obsession and the disappearing curriculum. *NEA Today*. https://scirp.org/reference/referencespapers.aspx?referenceid=1857098.

Winn, M.T. (2018). *Justice on both sides: Transforming education through restorative justice.* Harvard Education Press.

Chapter 9

Expanding Possibilities

Creating New Visions for Education

> "If you could wave a magic wand and change anything about the world, what would it be?"
>
> Interviewer

We close this book with a call for all of us to expand what we believe is possible in order to create new visions for education. At the core, the transformative process is a creative endeavor. We must first imagine and then create new possibilities for education—allowing ourselves to dream together with girls to build a new future. We seek not only to adjust a few school policies but to engage in deep transformation, including rethinking the purpose of education. Too many schools reflect a caretaker orientation in which educators believe children do not have the same rights as adults and that thus, adults must make decisions on their behalf and for their protection (Raby, 2012). Alternatively, we advocate for models of education that recognize the innate humanity of children, teach students how to be engaged citizens, listen to and honor the voices and experiences of children, and are willing and able to grow and adapt over time. We believe that "education at its best is always generative" (Ayers, 2016, p. 160).

Magic Wand

Educational models and practices which reinforce inequity are often self-perpetuating and can be difficult to change. People within these systems might come to believe that these approaches are inevitable. It is essential that we disrupt such hopelessness and failure of imagination in order to create spaces where students are safe and where they can grow as learners and as people. We offered students and educators we interviewed the opportunity to articulate their dreams and visions for transformation. We asked girls in our study what they would do if they had a magic wand and could change anything about the world. Grace (12th grade) articulated how gender equality would improve her quality of life:

DOI: 10.4324/9781003111535-10

> If I could change anything—oh, that would make my life so much better. But, in reality, if I could change one thing, [it] is that the opportunities for females were just as equal as [for] guys. I wouldn't have to worry about my future because I am a girl. I wouldn't have to worry about what this is going to look like. That I'll never be taken seriously in a relationship, that I will find someone that's going to fit me this way because I am a female. Like, half the time I wish I was born male because if I was born male, my life would be so good.

Girls advocated for equality in numerous ways that would extend far outside the educational realm. Laura (12th grade) answered, "Smash the patriarchy, bro." Eve (12th grade) said if she had a magic wand she would change, "Like, a racial standard, a wage standard, a gender standard, a sexuality standard. Just kind of let everybody do their own thing." April (12th grade) responded, "I think it would just be the basic human rights, where just—everyone had them."

Girls also shared visions for broader cultural change by shifting the distribution of power and resources in society. Rebecca (11th grade) shared that if she had a magic wand, she would change:

> the way people use power. Just because they—I think it gets to their head just the way we use things so wastefully and without a second thought. And we're not—especially like climate change, like, we're not thinking ahead, we're not thinking about taking care of our Earth.

Olivia (12th grade) talked about problems in society when a small group of people control the majority of the power and resources:

> I would change the distribution of power. I think that the biggest problem is that there's, like, so many people in poverty and then there is just this small percentage that has the world. And, I mean, even the people who are in the ... middle class, they're still big—I just feel like it's going further down, and I would change that definitely.

Isabel (12th grade) described what she would change if given a magic wand:

> I have a big problem with, like, religious wars—like, wars over religion. I don't know why but I have a huge issue with it. But I feel like going back to that acceptance of, like, we all believe—most people, unless you're atheist—but, like, most people believe in a god or multiple gods or a religious figure. And, like, we can all agree that we believe in a divine being or power, but, like, we're fighting and killing each other over this one thing that we also agree on. So, we have it in common but we're fighting and

> killing people and, like, we're fighting each other over it and it's like, *you* believe it, so allow other people to believe it.

Some of the girls we interviewed described their desire to change the way people behave towards others. Mya (11th grade) responded to the magic wand question by saying, "I would change the way we interact with each other ... that promotes self-growth and real connections, rather than just trying to superficially be accepted ... I want real connections with real relationships." Lisa (12th grade) said, "There is so much confusion in this world. Like, no one understands each other, and everyone is against each other." Elle (11th grade) said if she could change anything about the world:

> [I] would want it to be like more positive, 'cause there's a lot of, like, negativity going on, and there's, like, a lot of violence. And I would like that to, like—I know I can't stop it all the way but, like, a lot less, like the stuff in the Middle East, like ... I wish that would be like a lot less because it's terrible.

Nora (12th grade) described how changing interpersonal interactions could have larger ripple effects in society:

> I think just the kind of tension that goes on ... like, I wish there was more love and acceptance and just peace. Kind of get rid of the turmoil and people who are consumed with anger and that causes them to treat people differently. Just kind of make it nicer and happier.

The range and depth of responses from the girls we interviewed demonstrate how girls are engaging in the world and their awareness of social issues directly impacting their daily lives as well as global problems. Their answers also revealed that they have visions of a different world. They realize transformation is not easy or guaranteed, but it is possible. They articulated visions of a world with more equity, peace, love, and shared power and resources.

Hope Theory

Hope, and the idea of transformation, has been described, discussed, and identified throughout human history; however, the degree to which people believe that real transformation (of beliefs, systems, and individual attitudes) is possible has varied greatly. The most widely researched psychological construct of *hope theory* was developed by C.R. Snyder in the 1990s and looks at hope from a cognitive perspective (Lopez, Pedrotti, and Snyder, 2019). According to this model, hope is made up of goal-directed thoughts, pathways, and agency. Pathways are routes to the things one wishes for (goals), and agency is the motivation to actively pursue the different routes towards those goals and cope with barriers or setbacks along the way. Developmentally speaking, pathways are the cognitive understanding of cause and effect, and agency is one's ability to act. It is important to note that Snyder (2000) found that hope is not something we are born with, but it is something that we learn, as young children, from parents and adults in our lives.

Brené Brown summarizes hope theory as follows: hope is the result of realistic goals, coming up with different ways to achieve those goals, and believing one can pursue their goals (Brown, 2010, p. 66). Furthermore, Brown (2010) points out that while perseverance is an important component of being hopeful, so is flexibility—the goals that make up hope can and will look different, and the effort, energy, and emotion put forth to achieve those goals also varies. In her research, Brown has found that resilience and hope are important ingredients for individual well-being as well as working toward systemic transformation. It is crucial to acknowledge the role that oppression, white supremacy, and privilege play in the expression and suppression of hope among those who have been systemically discriminated against and oppressed. Researchers have described the importance of scaffolding and supporting hope among marginalized groups, particularly youth (Nerenberg, 2019). Dixson (2019) points out that lack of messages about the possibility of academic achievement, lack of representation across academically-rigorous disciplines, and lowered expectations for marginalized youth contribute to the academic achievement gap in the United States. Hope interventions, on the other hand, help students see and imagine possibilities, positively increase motivation to achieve those goals and dreams, and problem-solve potential barriers to those goals (Nerenberg, 2019). "Where is hope and positivity in American educational policy? Cheap, effective, and scalable interventions centered around these concepts improve student achievement, student mental health, and school discipline records" (Dixson, 2019, p. 130). Dixson and Stevens (2018) found that hope was statistically related to scholastic achievement variables in their study of African American students. Dixson (2019) is not trying to minimize the impact of structural racism on students from historically marginalized groups; rather, he points to racism's power to diminish hope (which can be promoted at both the individual and the collective levels) and how hopelessness negatively impacts the likelihood of collective action (Aubin et al., 2016).

Bryant-Davis has written extensively on the promotion of hope, meaning-making, and post-traumatic growth in response to trauma including traumatic experiences such as sexual abuse, war, intergenerational trauma, racism, and oppression (Bryant-Davis and Wong, 2013). Bryant-Davis and colleagues call for hope and healing via attention to the religious and spiritual practices of those who have been traumatized, as well as through culturally sensitive, trauma-informed, empowerment-based programs through the lens of a womanist framework (Bryant-Davis and Gobin, 2019). Scholars have also described a psychological framework of radical hope that integrates hope theory with radical healing and racial and ethnic studies (Mosley et al., 2019). Drawing on the work of Lear (2006), radical hope combines a belief in the possibility of positive change at the collective level with an awareness of systemic and historic barriers in communities of color. The four pathways to radical hope outlined by Mosley et al. (2019) include an understanding of the history of oppression, resistance and transformation, "embracing ancestral pride" (p. 1), the ability to imagine or envision equitable possibilities, and social justice as a route to meaning and purpose. Though it is beyond the scope of this chapter, French et al. (2020) have written about a psychological, multi-system framework for radical healing that has radical hope as one of the root constructs.

Our Joys, Our Sorrows, Our Visions

Throughout this project, we have been impacted by the words of the girls and educators we worked with. Our intention throughout our work is to be more expansive in our understanding of girls' lives. We are often left with as many questions as answers. Here we detail the aspects of this project that brought us joy, our moments of sorrow, and our visions for educational transformation.

Britney G. Brinkman, PhD

Throughout this project, I experienced many moments of hope and joy while listening to young women articulate their lived experiences with passion, clarity, and nuance. I was inspired by the ways girls navigated challenging situations and oppressive systems with creativity, dedication, and grace. I also felt deep sorrow, anger, and hopelessness when I heard girls' stories of sexism, sexual violence, racism, and the failure of adults to intervene. However, I remain hopeful and believe that we can transform educational systems into places where all students (and educators) can thrive. I remain committed to working for this transformation, to center girls' dreams for themselves and others, and to shine a light on the visions of a different kind of schooling.

Kandie Brinkman, PhD

My greatest joy discovered in doing this project is that young women find value in their Catholic education. At times, I lost sight of my primary objective for this study—to explore how the best of Catholic principles create resiliency for girls. In their spirituality, they can discover the goodness of self and act on this truth. My sorrow is that things haven't changed very much over the years we completed this project. Girls in Phase 1 and Phase 2 faced major acts of sexism and male privilege. It is heartbreaking to hear the many times they encountered male entitlement through sexism and racism. My vision is to continue to unmask the multiple ways boys and men move women from the center and in doing so, firmly place our story in the forefront of social interaction, change, and—most importantly—school. As a social justice researcher and educator, I look to the horizon to see the hope these girls bring to social transformation.

Deanna Hamilton, PhD

My greatest joy in this project was getting to hear the stories of so many amazing women and girls, including the students and teachers we interviewed, my co-authors, and the coding team who worked on this project. Getting to really, deeply listen to your experiences, to see you a little more clearly, to know your stories more fully, was a gift. I learned so much.

My greatest sorrow was sitting with the painful stories we heard from so many girls and not being able to fix them. *And* my vision for the future is based on the hope and resilience in their stories and experiences. Our participants convinced me that transformation is possible and the girls—as well as the adults who support them—need space, resources, and compassion for that transformation to take place.

Looking To the Horizon

What is next for education? We do not expect educational transformation to happen quickly or easily. But we do believe it can—and should—happen. In addition to setting realistic and immediate goals for changing school systems, we argue that we need to look to the horizon for what education *can* be and commit to take steps toward that vision.

In this book, we challenged some traditional definitions of resilience and how it has been used to limit girls' ability to thrive. However, we are not advocating that schools abandon all notions of resilience, but rather rethink how they use this construct. Resilience can mean being flexible and adapting to one's circumstances. "Resilience is learning to dance with life, to flex, adapt, and create as life keeps surprising us" (Frieze and Wheatley, 2011, p. 126). We believe schools should support girls in becoming resilient but should not ask them to just become more resilient to oppression—especially the oppression that is happening within the school itself. Resilience grows in communities and through relationships. It manifests when systems support people through their challenges and adversity. And we know that girls will face adversity in their lives—not just because of their experiences of oppression but also as they navigate the challenges of being human.

We want girls to have the resilience to move through life's challenges and grow as a result. And we worry that many girls are struggling in ways that are invisible or dismissed by the adults in their lives. The pressures to be good, smart, and/or super are taking their toll on girls. Many are doing everything they can to rise to these challenges despite the adverse impacts on their own well-being. Too often, educators see only the strength that Super Girls possess and then dismiss and minimize their needs. We recognize that survival dissonance is an understandable (and perhaps inevitable) result of being stuck in oppressive systems. We also worry about the negative consequences of learning how to survive in adverse situations. We must allow girls to be fully human—to succeed and achieve and also to make mistakes and need support. We cannot continue to treat resilience as the solution to systemic oppression; instead, we need to shift our focus to changing the systems that are harming girls.

We were amazed by the myriad strategies that girls utilized to engage in resistance to oppression. We encourage this continued resistance and we need to change the contexts in which girls learn to resist. As we and other scholars have described, the precarious nature of manhood and the fear of not measuring up leads many boys and men to engage in destructive and harmful behaviors, including their interactions with girls in schools. We collected data over more than a decade in schools and saw how toxic versions of masculinity pervaded school climates and persisted. In fact, in some ways, this aspect of the girls' experience became worse. While some boys and men do support girls' equality, and many boys desire changes in the culture related to masculinity (toxic masculinity harms them as well), most of our schools continue to accommodate, make excuses for, apologize for, or even promote harmful versions of masculinity.

What sits on the horizon is a world in which we challenge restrictive, binary notions of gender. A world in which we hold boys and men responsible for their own feelings, needs, and behavior. On our horizon, sit school systems that do not reinforce toxic masculinity or create permissive environments rooted in notions that educators are too helpless to intervene. We wonder about the potential for what girls could do and be if they didn't have to waste their energy avoiding the thin ice of fragile masculinity. Feeling safe in school should not be a privilege afforded to a few groups of students but should be the expectation for all students.

Activism is one important avenue for creating change in schools. We advocate for activism and advocacy efforts which center the experiences and voices of girls (and students of all gender identities). Youth activism makes waves that are bigger than the immediate outcomes—which might or might not be what students hope for. Engaging in these efforts can be transformative for the girls themselves and can plant seeds for long-term change. Educators can provide support and scaffolding for students engaging in this transformative work. We also recognize the necessity of healing for educators and support for activist teachers—making schools spaces for all students to thrive should not come at the expense of the well-being of educators.

There are many pathways for educational transformation—we have shared some of them in this book. We encourage you, the reader, to choose a pathway and start walking toward your horizon of equitable schools. Each step matters. Every small change is important. We can transform schools and students' experiences within them if we are brave enough to dream of a new vision of what education can be and persevere in bringing those dreams to life.

References

Ayers, B. (2016). *Demand the impossible!: A radical manifesto*. Haymarket Books.

Aubin, R.M., Amiot, C.E., and Fontaine-Boyte, C. (2016). The impact of group power and its perceived stability on hope and collective action: Applying the concept of hopelessness at the collective level of analysis. *Group Dynamics: Theory, Research, and Practice*, 20(2), 105. doi:10.1037/gdn0000045.

Brown, B. (2010). *The gifts of imperfection: Let go of who you think you're supposed to be and embrace who you are*. Hazelden Publishing.

Bryant-Davis, T. and Gobin, R.L. (2019). Still we rise: Psychotherapy for African American girls and women exiting sex trafficking. *Women & Therapy*, 42(3–4),385–405. doi:10.1080/02703149.2019.1622902.

Bryant-Davis, T. and Wong, E.C. (2013). Faith to move mountains: Religious coping, spirituality, and interpersonal trauma recovery. *American Psychologist*, 68(8), 675–684. doi:10.1037/a0034380.

Dixson, D.D. (2019). Incorporating hope and positivity into educational policy. *Policy Insights from the Behavioral and Brain Sciences*, 6(2), 130–137. doi:10.1177/2372732219863137.

Dixson, D.D. and Stevens, D. (2018). A potential avenue for academic success: Hope predicts an achievement-oriented psychosocial profile in African American adolescents. *Journal of Black Psychology*, 44(6), 532–561. doi:10.1177/0095798418805644.

French, B.H.et al. (2020). Toward a psychological framework of radical healing in communities of color. *The Counseling Psychologist*, 48(1), 14–46. doi:10.1177%2F0011000019843506.

Frieze, D. and Wheatley, M. (2011). *Walk out, walk on*. Berrett-Koehler Publishers.

Lear, J. (2006). *Radical hope: Ethics in the face of cultural devastation*. Harvard University Press.

Lopez, S.J., Pedrotti, J.T., and Snyder, C.R. (2018). *Positive psychology: The scientific and practical explorations of human strengths*. Sage Publications.

Mosley, D.V.et al. (2019). Radical hope in revolting times: Proposing a culturally relevant psychological framework. *Social and Personality Psychology Compass*, 14 (1), 1–12. doi:10.1111/spc3.12512.

Nerenberg, J. (2019, May 31). Why marginalized students need hope to succeed. *Greater Good Magazine*. https://greatergood.berkeley.edu/article/item/why_marginalized_students_need_hope_to_succeed.

Raby, R. (2012). *School rules: Obedience, discipline, and elusive democracy*. University of Toronto Press.

Snyder, C.R. (2000). The past and possible futures of hope. *Journal of Social and Clinical Psychology*, 19(1), 11–28. doi:10.1521/jscp.2000.19.1.11.

Appendices

Appendix A

Student Participants

Participants	*Name of attending School*	*Grade*	*Ethnicity*
Phase 1			
Mia	St. Bernadette Catholic School	6th-8th	African-American
Pammy	St. Bernadette Catholic School	6th-9th	White
Kathleen	St. Bernadette Catholic School	6th-8th	Latina
Emma	St. Bernadette Catholic School	6th-8th	White
Danna	St. Bernadette Catholic School	6th-8th	White
Alyssa	St. Bernadette Catholic School	6th-8th	Multi-ethnic
Hanna	St. Bernadette Catholic School	6th-8th	White
Sloan	St. Bernadette Catholic School and Christ the King Catholic High School	6th-9th &11th	White
Molly	St. Bernadette Catholic School and Christ the King Catholic High School	6th-9th &11th	Latina
Olivia	St. Bernadette Catholic School and Christ the King Catholic High School	6th-9th	Asian American
Alana	St. Bernadette Catholic School	6th-8th	Latina
Phase 2			
Joy	Our Lady of Guadalupe Catholic High School	12th	White
Grace	Our Lady of Guadalupe Catholic High School	12th	White
Maria	Our Lady of Guadalupe Catholic High School	12th	Latina
Rebecca	Our Lady of Guadalupe Catholic High School	12th	White
Diedre	Our Lady of Guadalupe Catholic High School	12th	White

Participants	*Name of attending School*	*Grade*	*Ethnicity*
Olivia	Our Lady of Guadalupe Catholic High School	12th	Latina
Eve	Our Lady of Guadalupe Catholic High School	12th	White
Lisa	Our Lady of Guadalupe Catholic High School	12th	East Indian
Tina	Our Lady of Guadalupe Catholic High School	12th	White
Nora	Our Lady of Guadalupe Catholic High School	12th	White
Laura	Our Lady of Guadalupe Catholic High School	12th	White
April	Our Lady of Guadalupe Catholic High School	12th	White
Carrie	Our Lady of Guadalupe Catholic High School	11th	White
Elle	Our Lady of Guadalupe Catholic High School	11th	White
Ava	Our Lady of Guadalupe Catholic High School	12th	White
Myah	Our Lady of Guadalupe Catholic High School	11th	Asian American
Rose	Our Lady of Guadalupe Catholic High School	12th	Latina
Erin	Our Lady of Guadalupe Catholic High School	11th	White
Isabel	Our Lady of Guadalupe Catholic High School	12th	White
Mia	Our Lady of Guadalupe Catholic High School	11th	White

Appendix B: Educator Participants

Participant	*School*	*Gender*	*Ethnicity*	*Years as an Educator*
Mrs. Carter	Our Lady of Guadalupe Catholic High School	Female	White	20
Ms. Lewis	Our Lady of Guadalupe Catholic High School	Female	White	17
Mr. Walker	Our Lady of Guadalupe Catholic High School	Male	White	3
Mr. Hill	Christ the King Catholic High School	Male	White	18
Ms. Powell	Our Lady of Guadalupe Catholic High School	Female	Latina	19
Ms. Jackson	Our Lady of Guadalupe Catholic High School	Female	White	
Miss Jones	St. Martin de Porres	Female	White	8
Mrs. Green	St. Martin de Porres	Female	White	
Mr. Baker	Our Lady of Guadalupe Catholic High School	Male	White	5
Mrs. Moore	Our Lady of Guadalupe Catholic High School	Female	White	11
Dr. Wilson	Christ the King Catholic High School	Female	White	11
Mrs. Smith	Our Lady of Guadalupe Catholic High School	Female	White	18

Index